Mindfulness Escapes

Adult Coloring Book

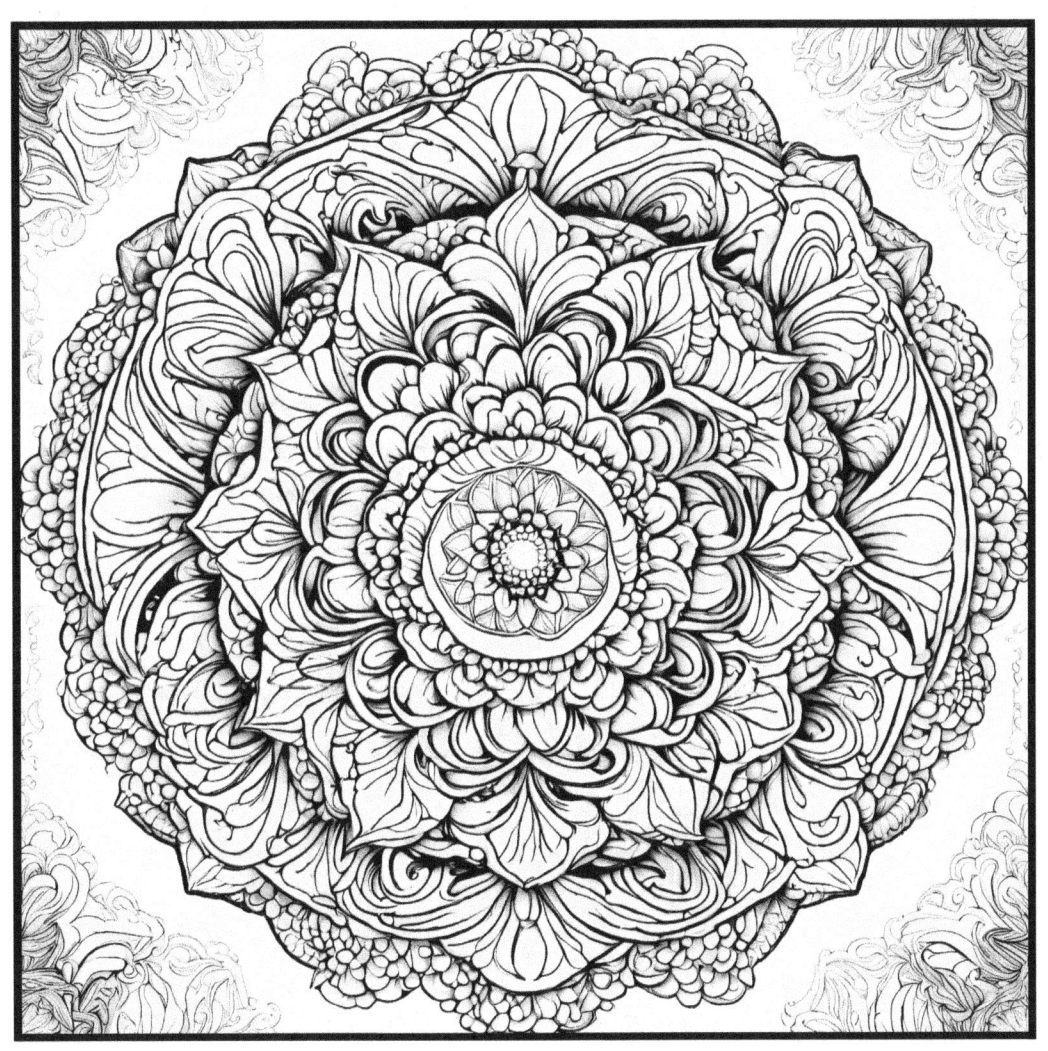

Part of the Mandala Magic series

Brooke E. Morgan

Thank you for purchasing this coloring book and embracing your creativity while finding moments of calm. Filled with delightful images, these pages offer a canvas for your artistic joy. I trust you'll enjoy crafting beautiful scenes that evoke the carefree bliss of childhood days.

Sincerely,

Brooke

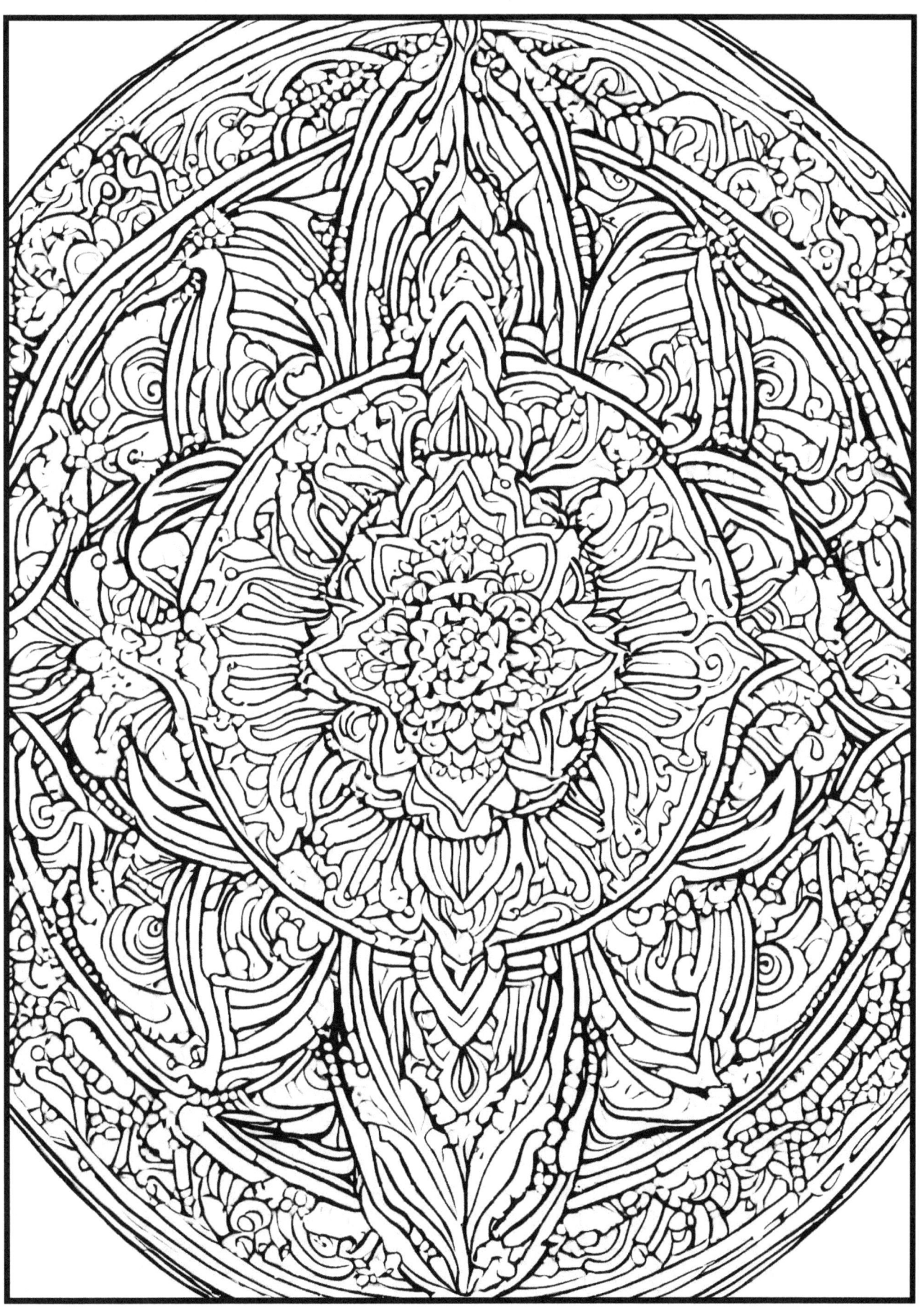

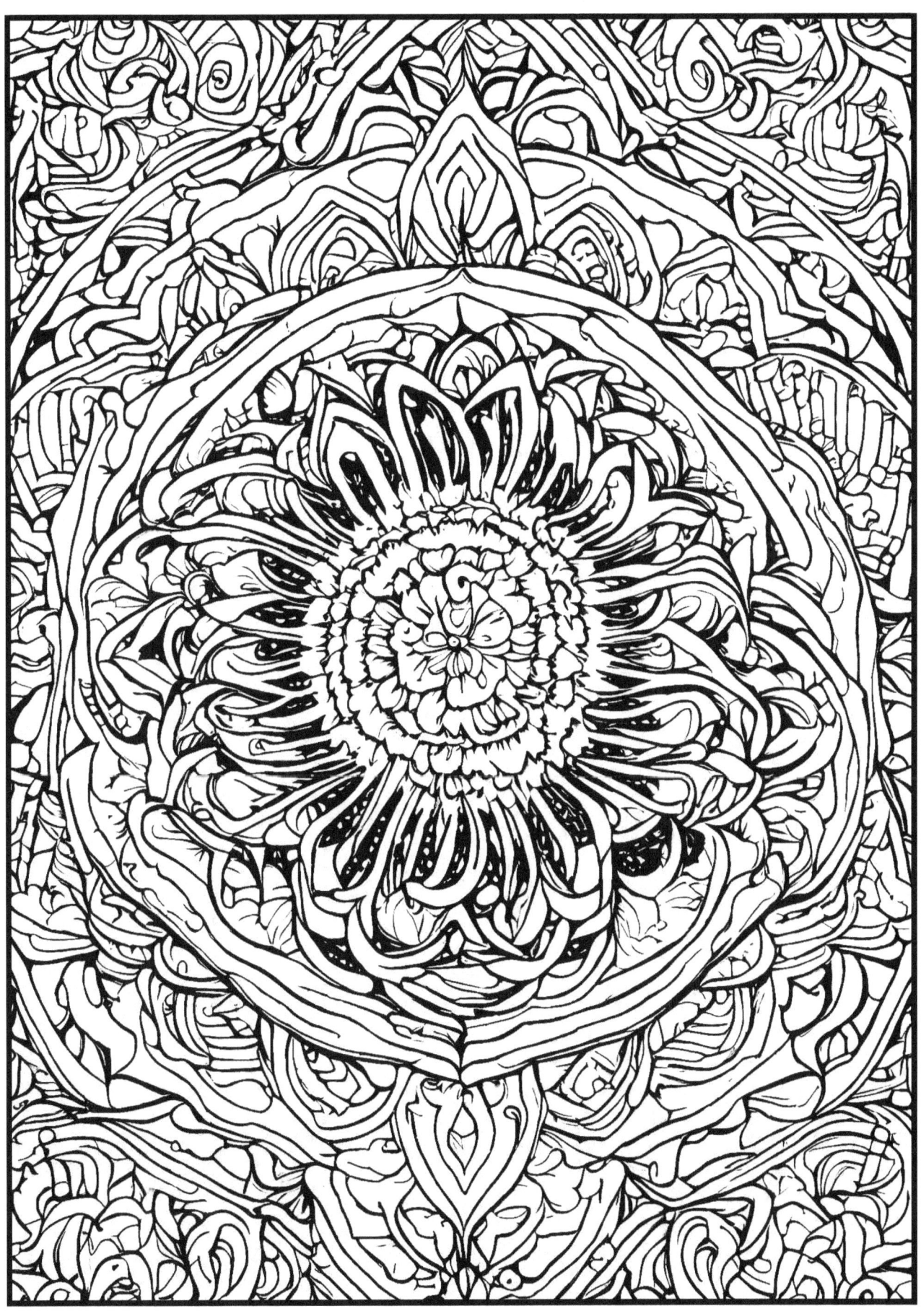

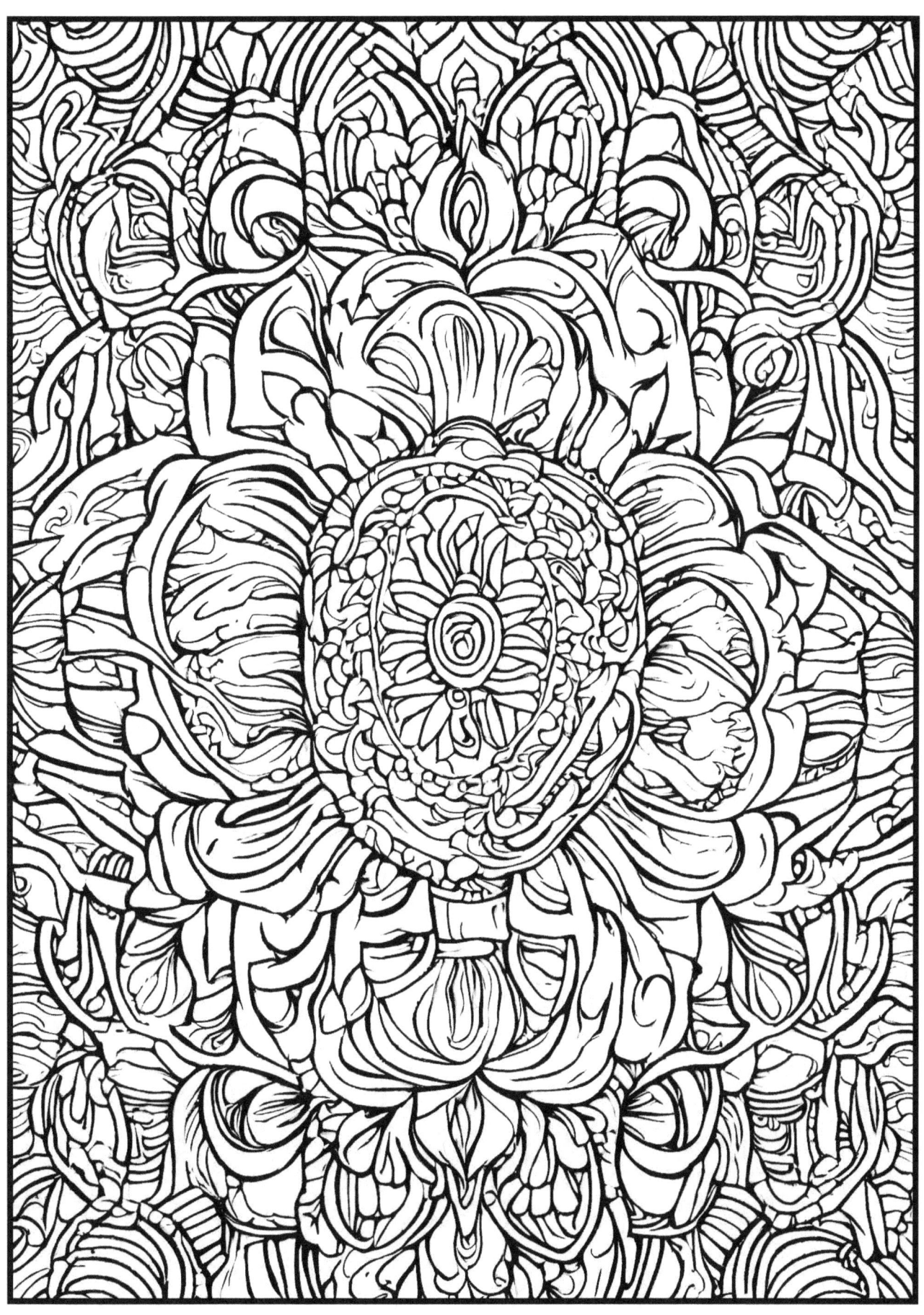

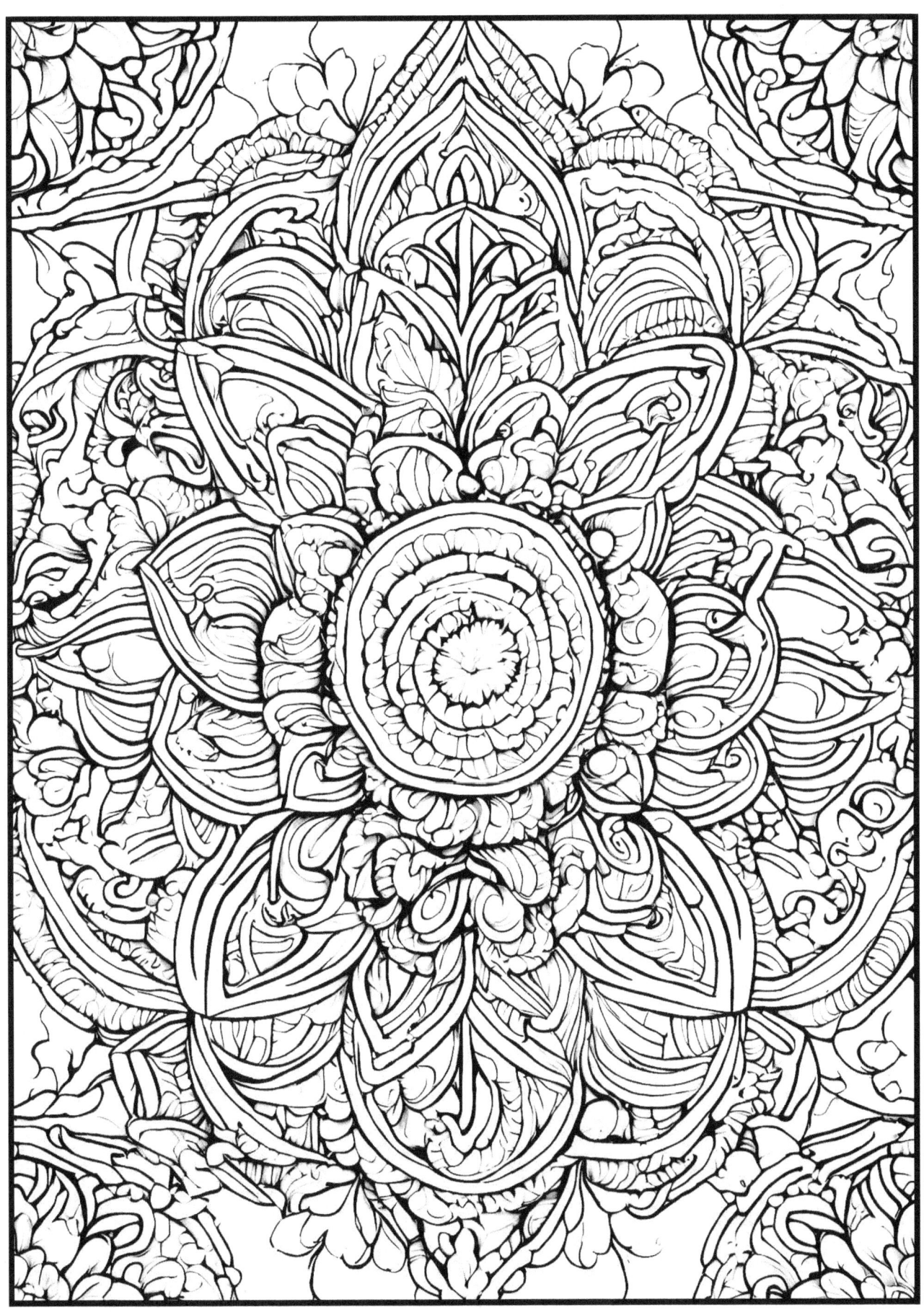

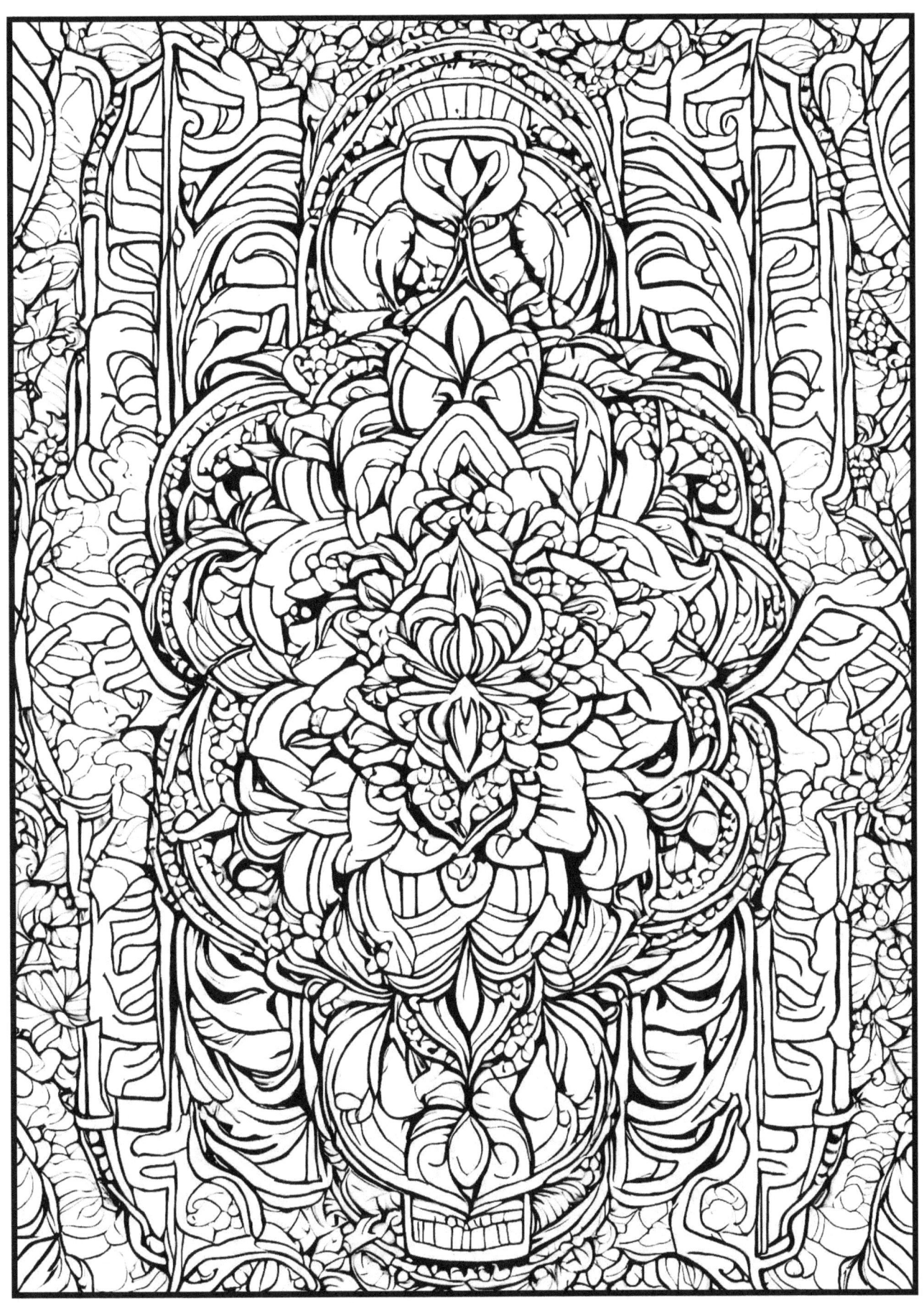

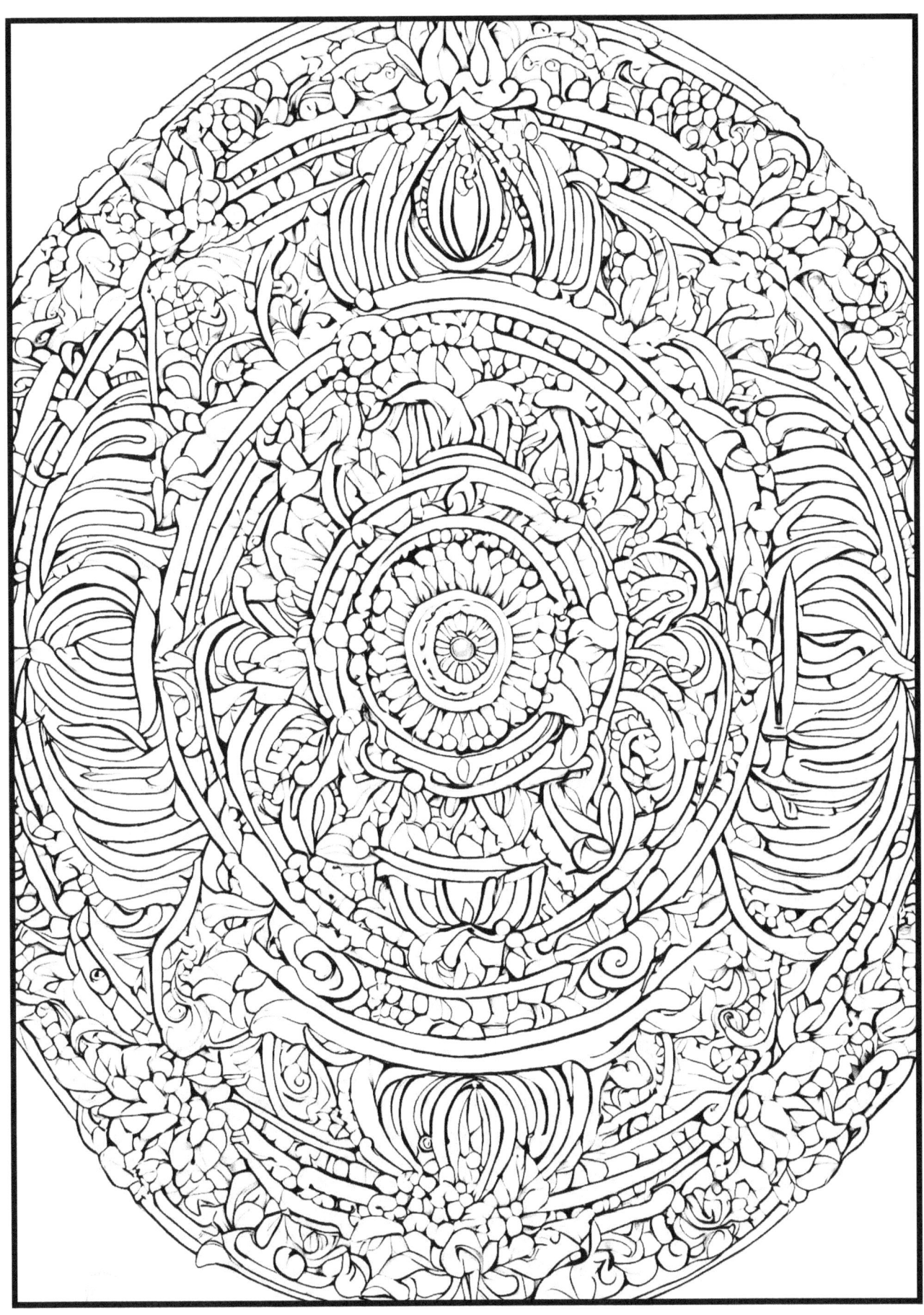

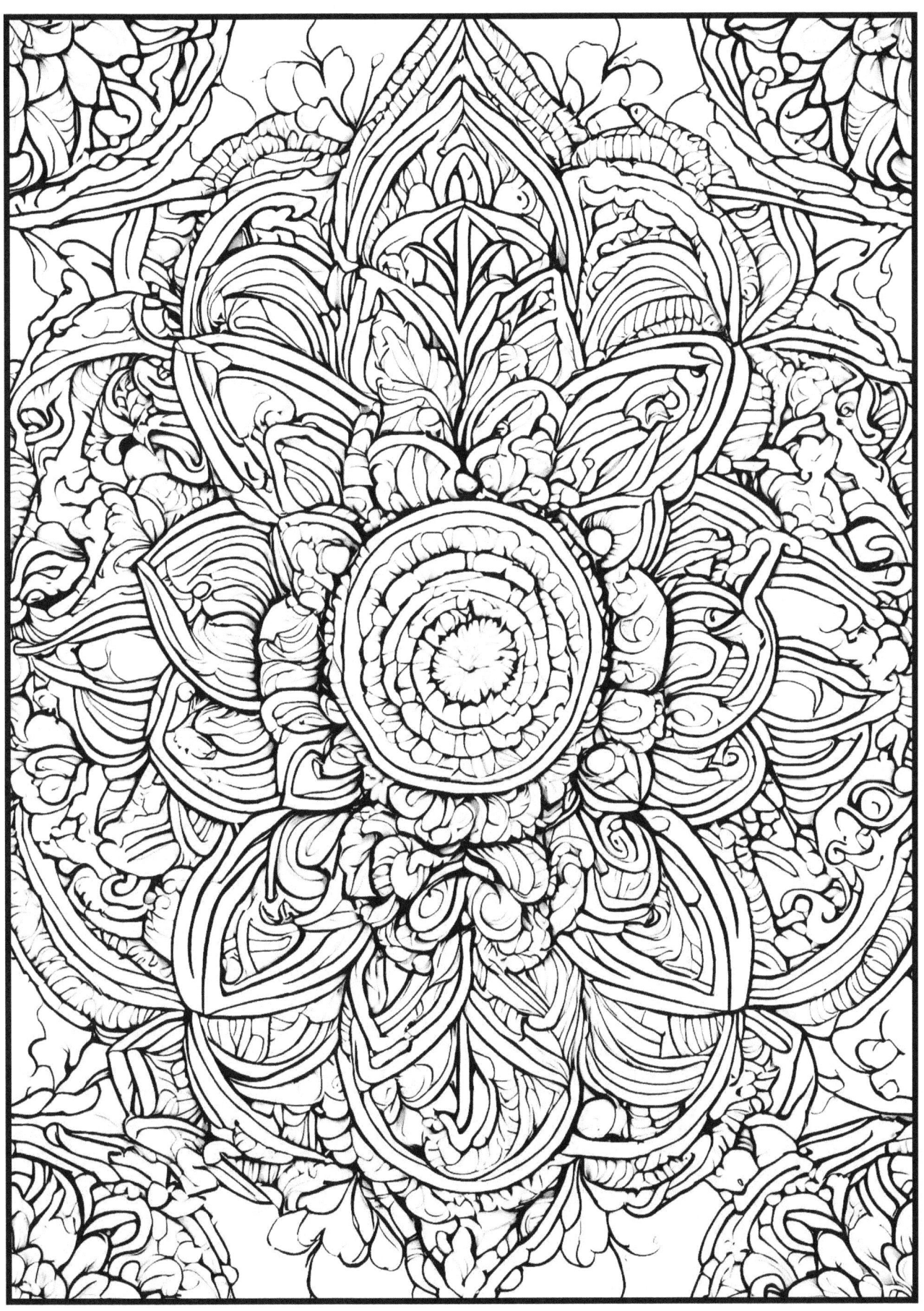

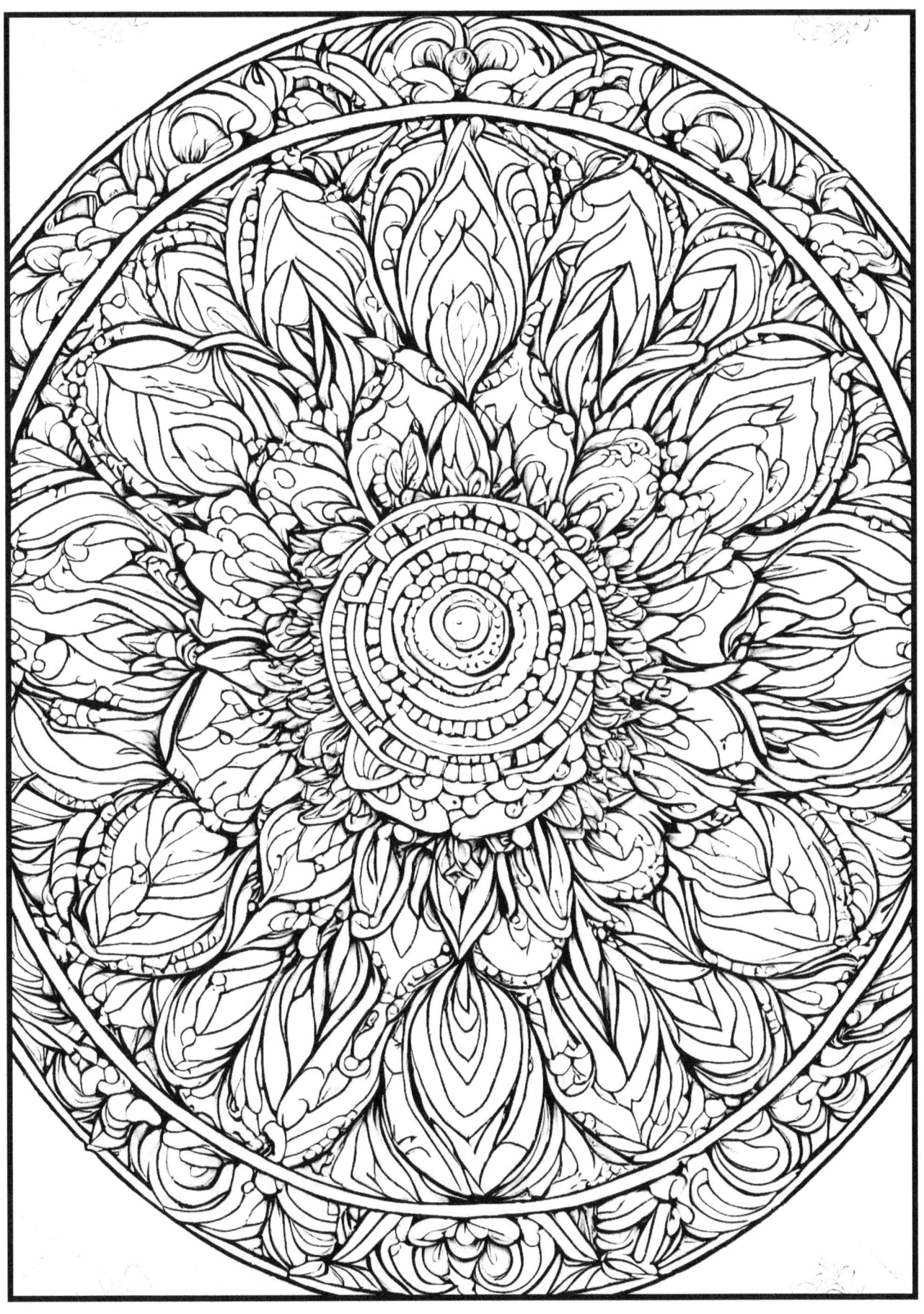

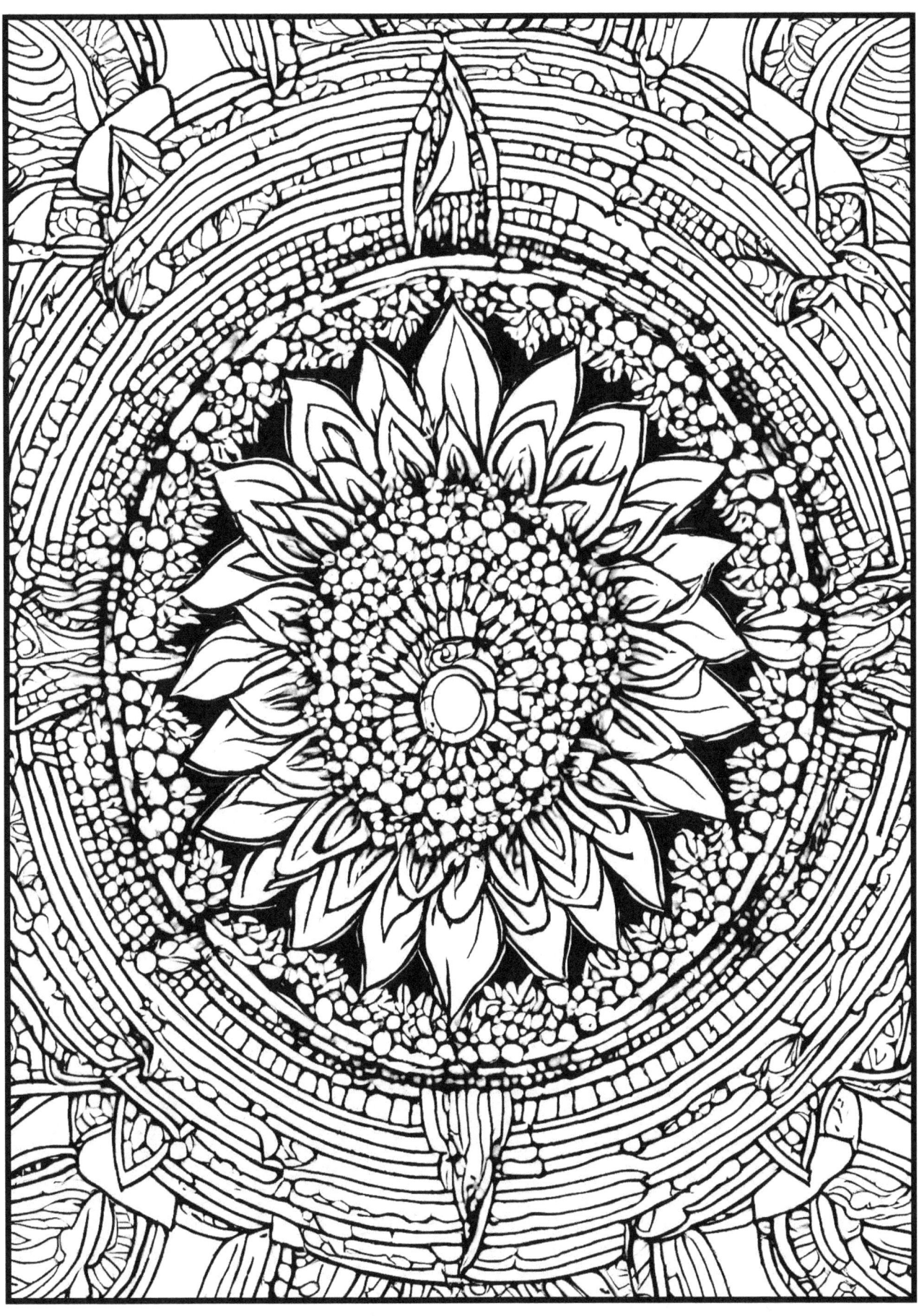

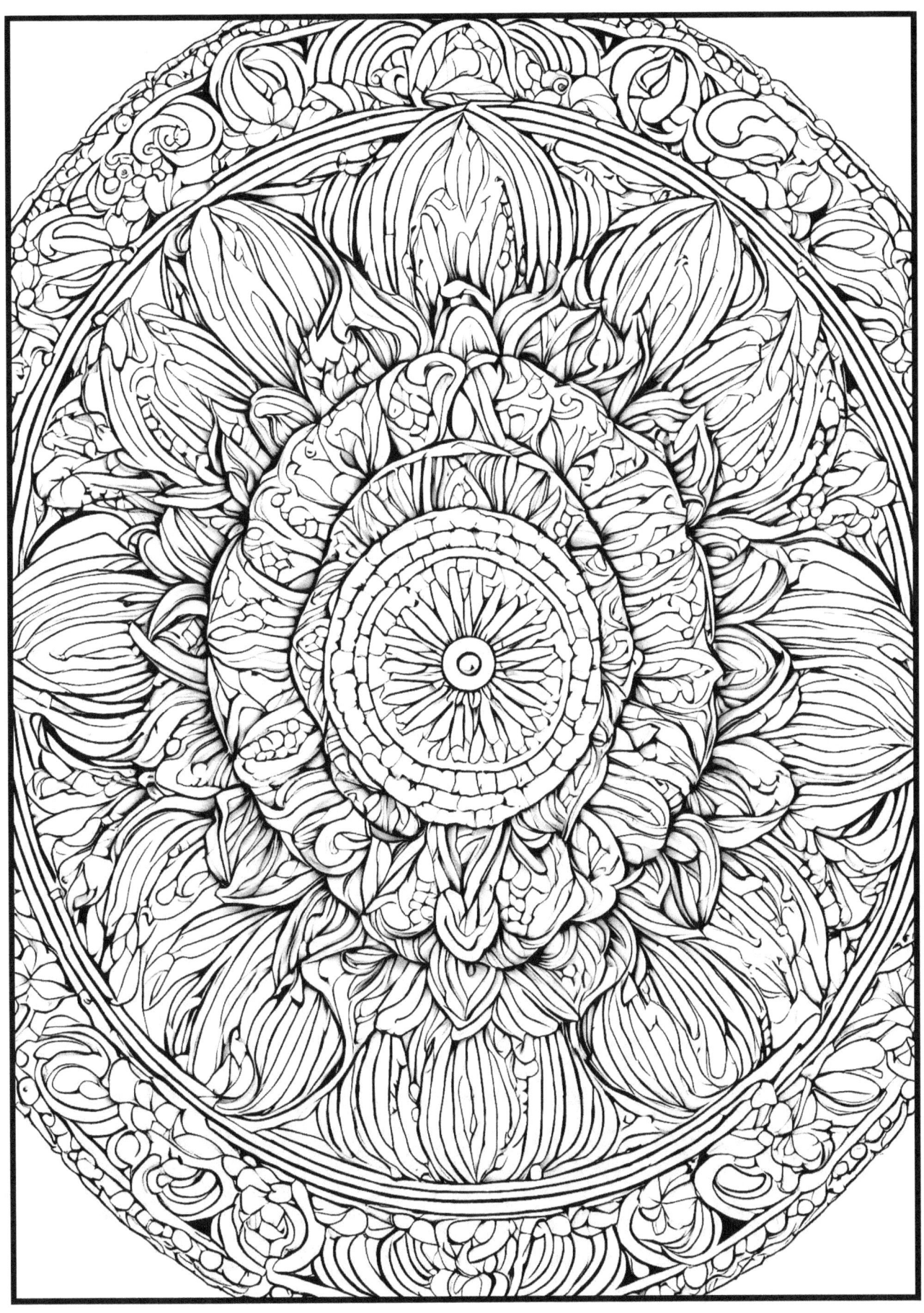

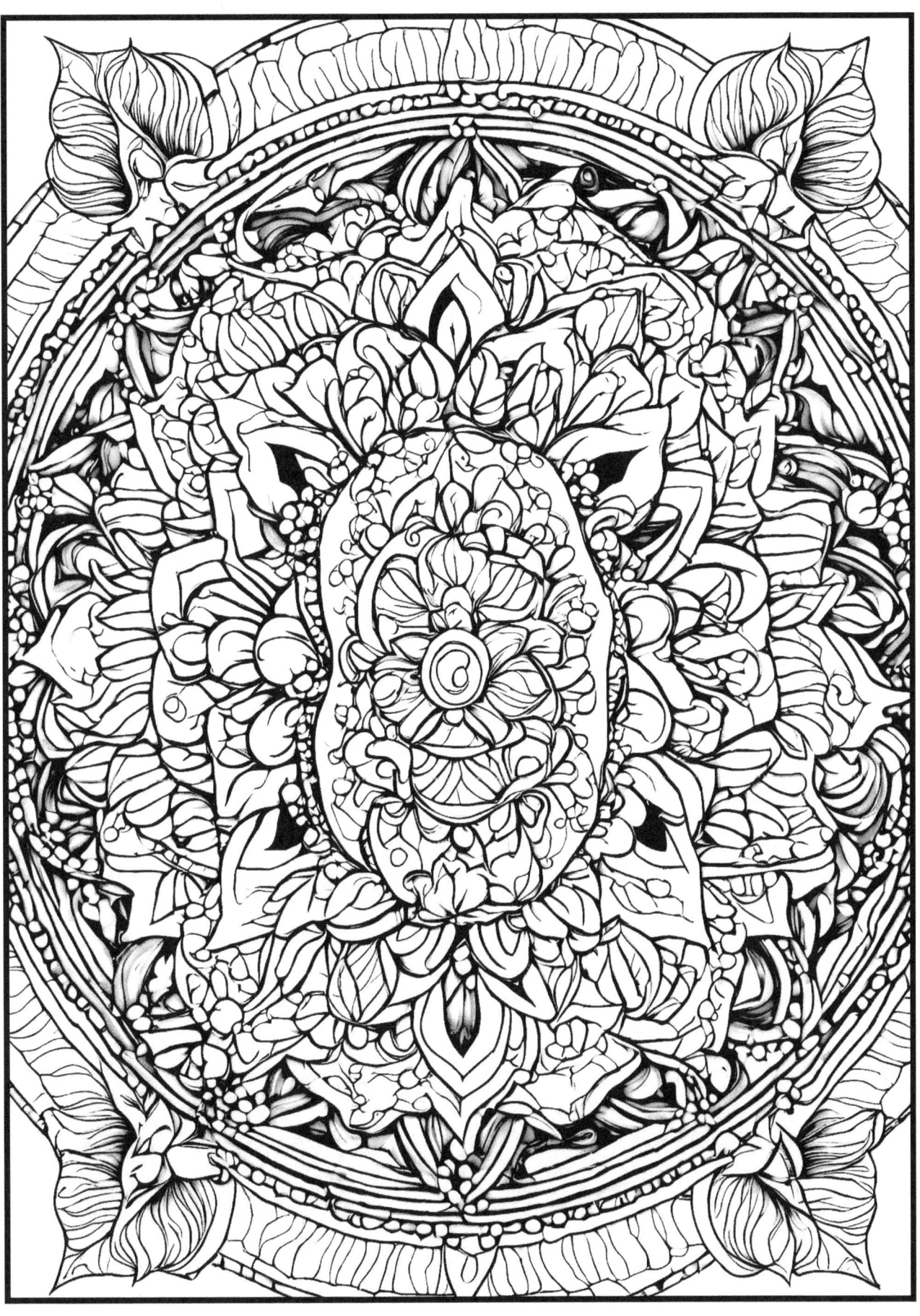

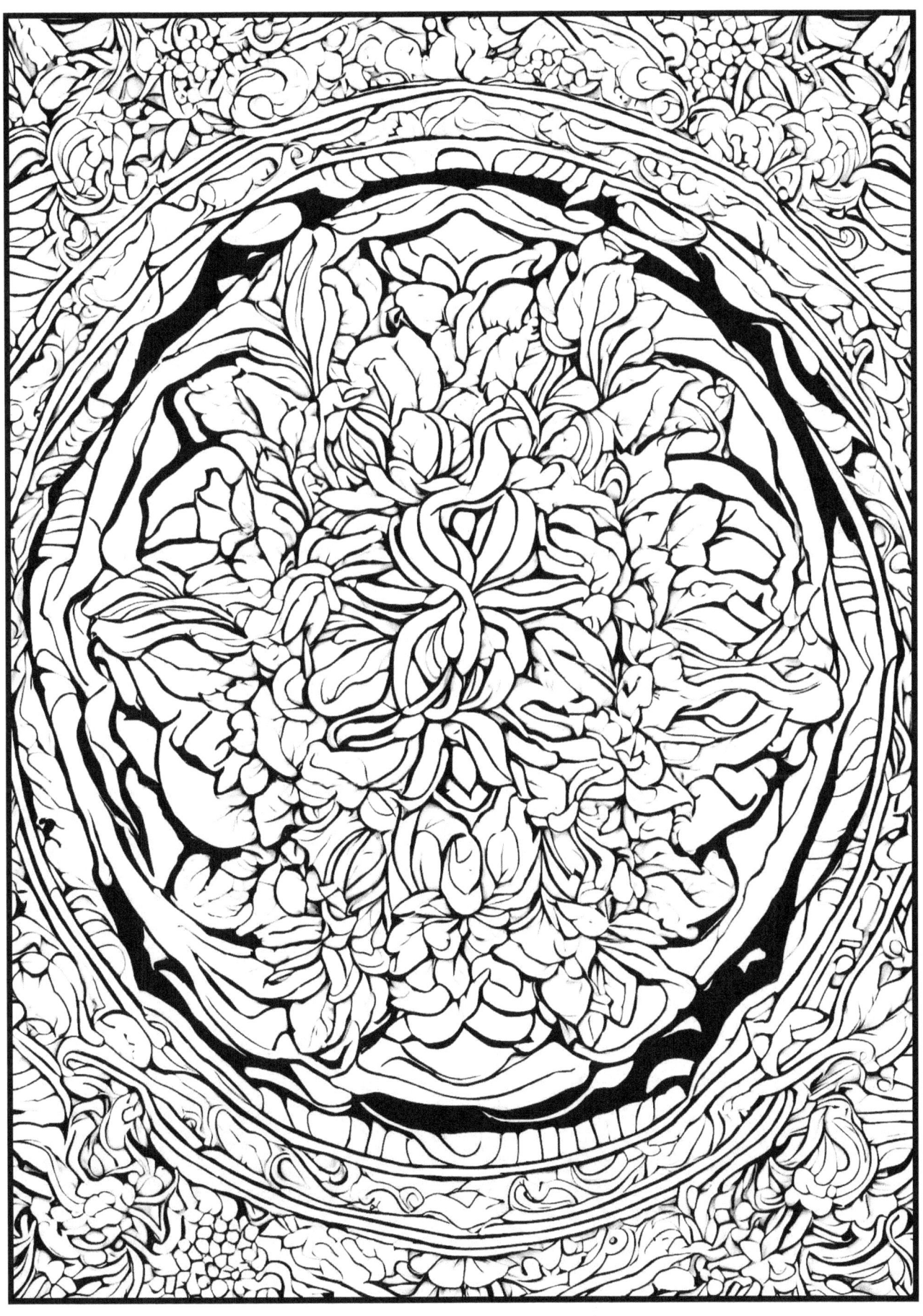

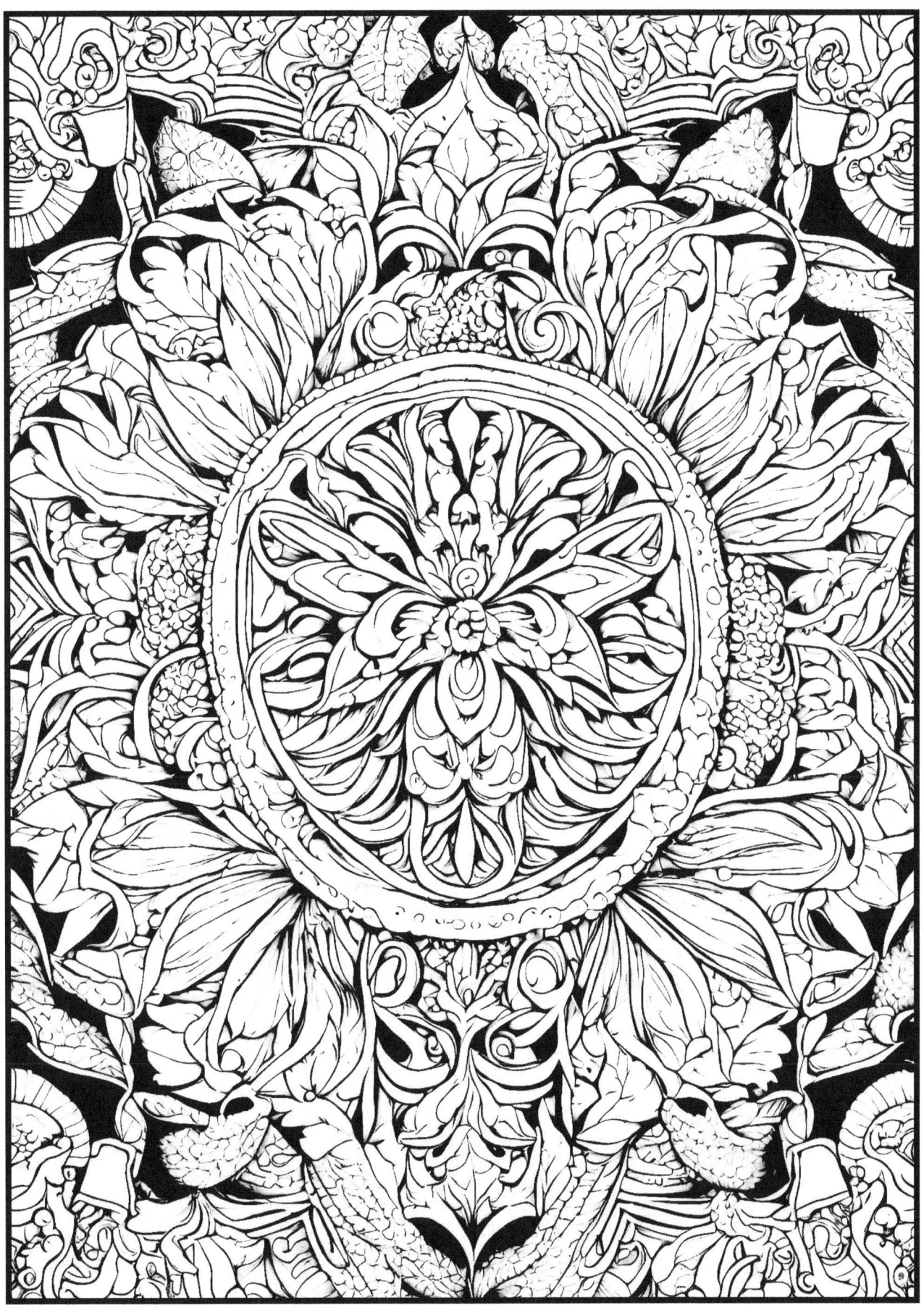

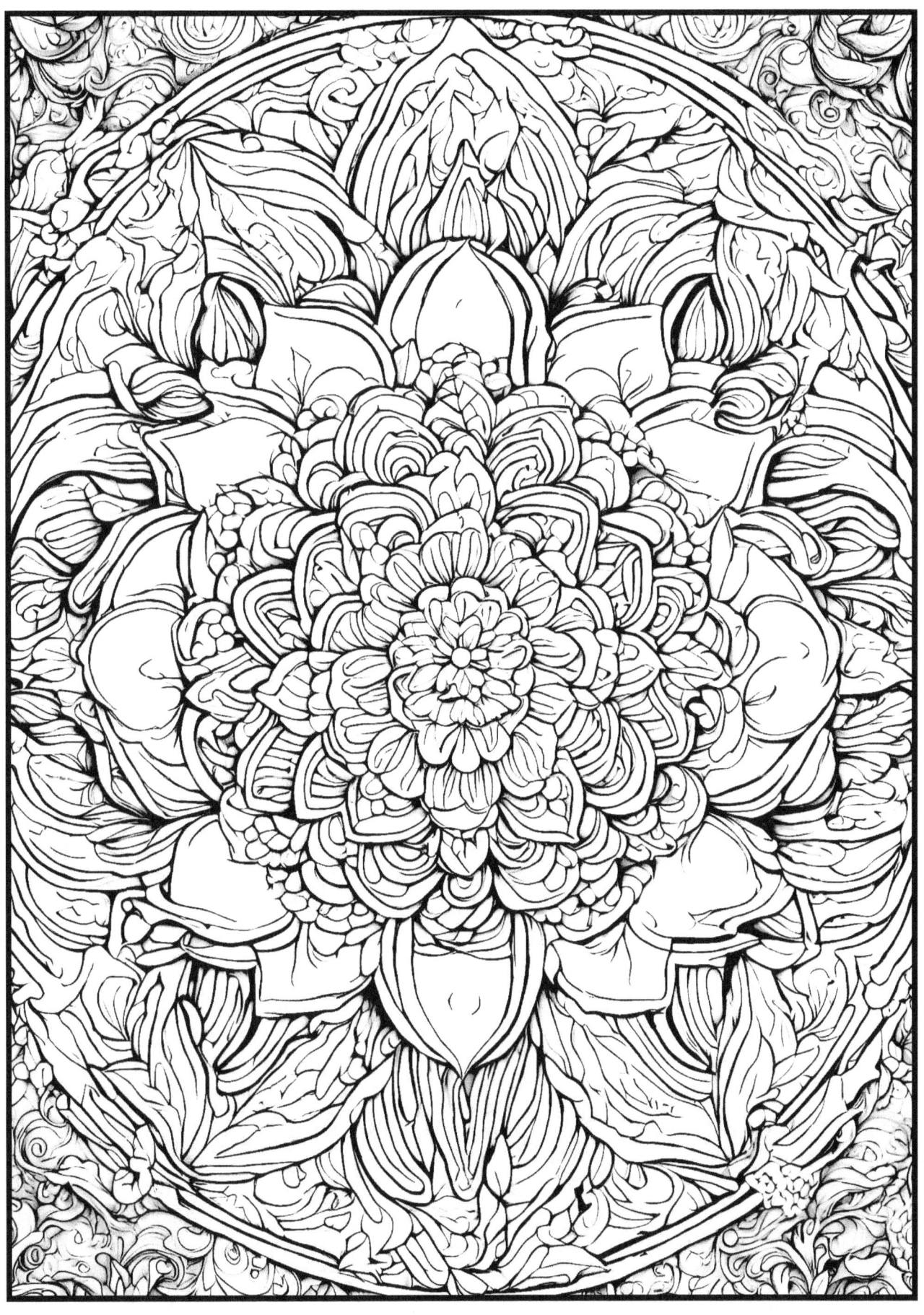

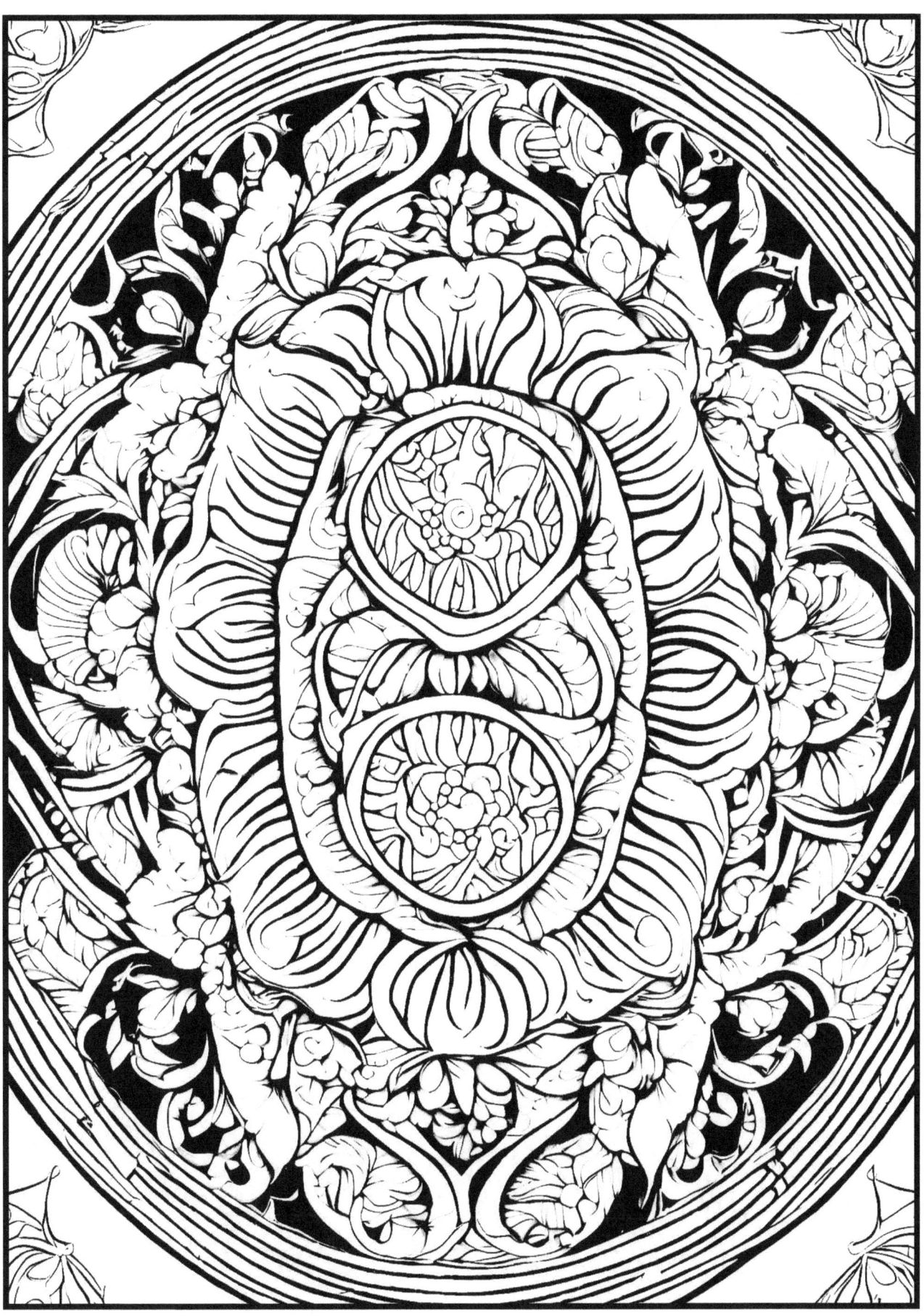

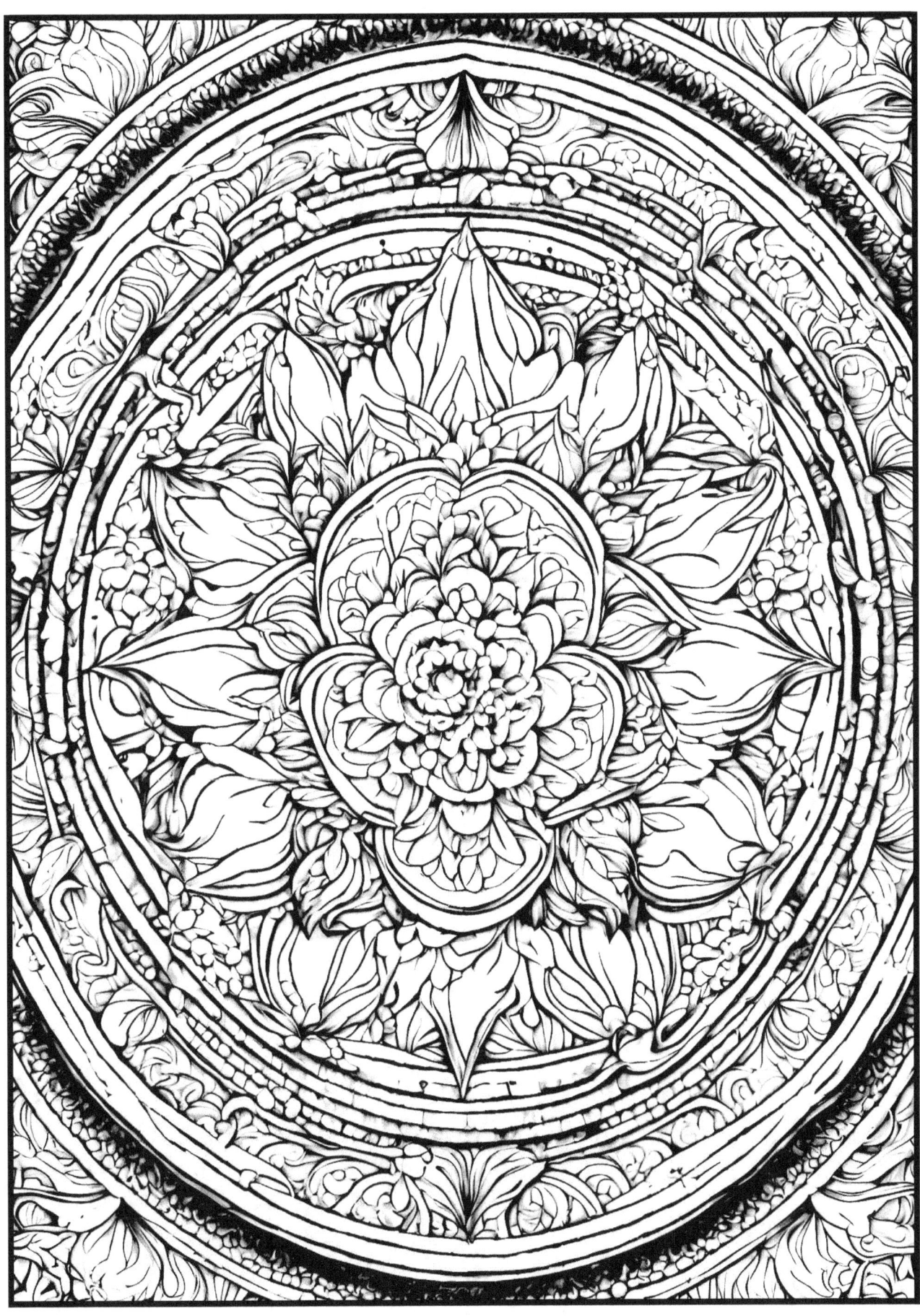

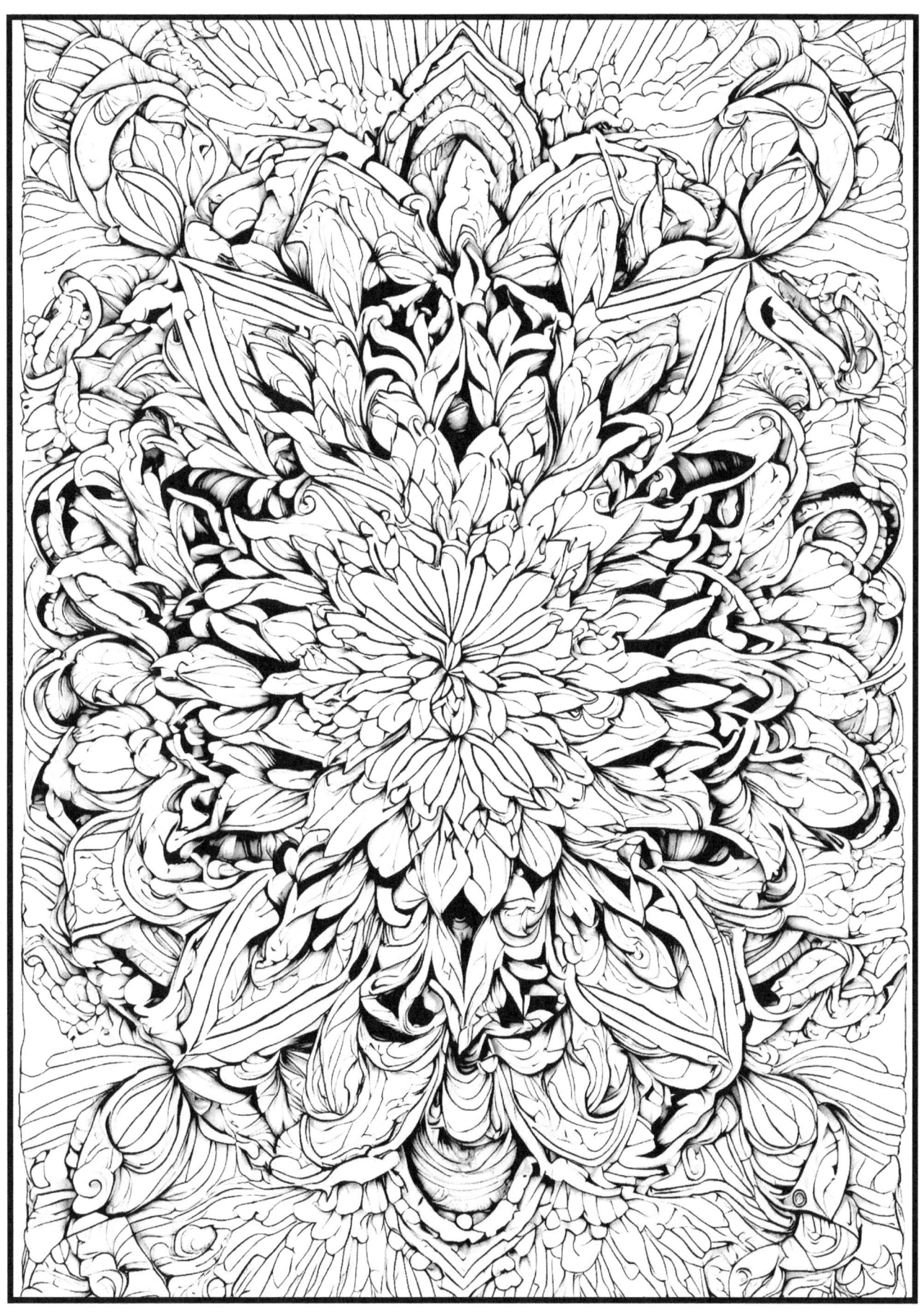

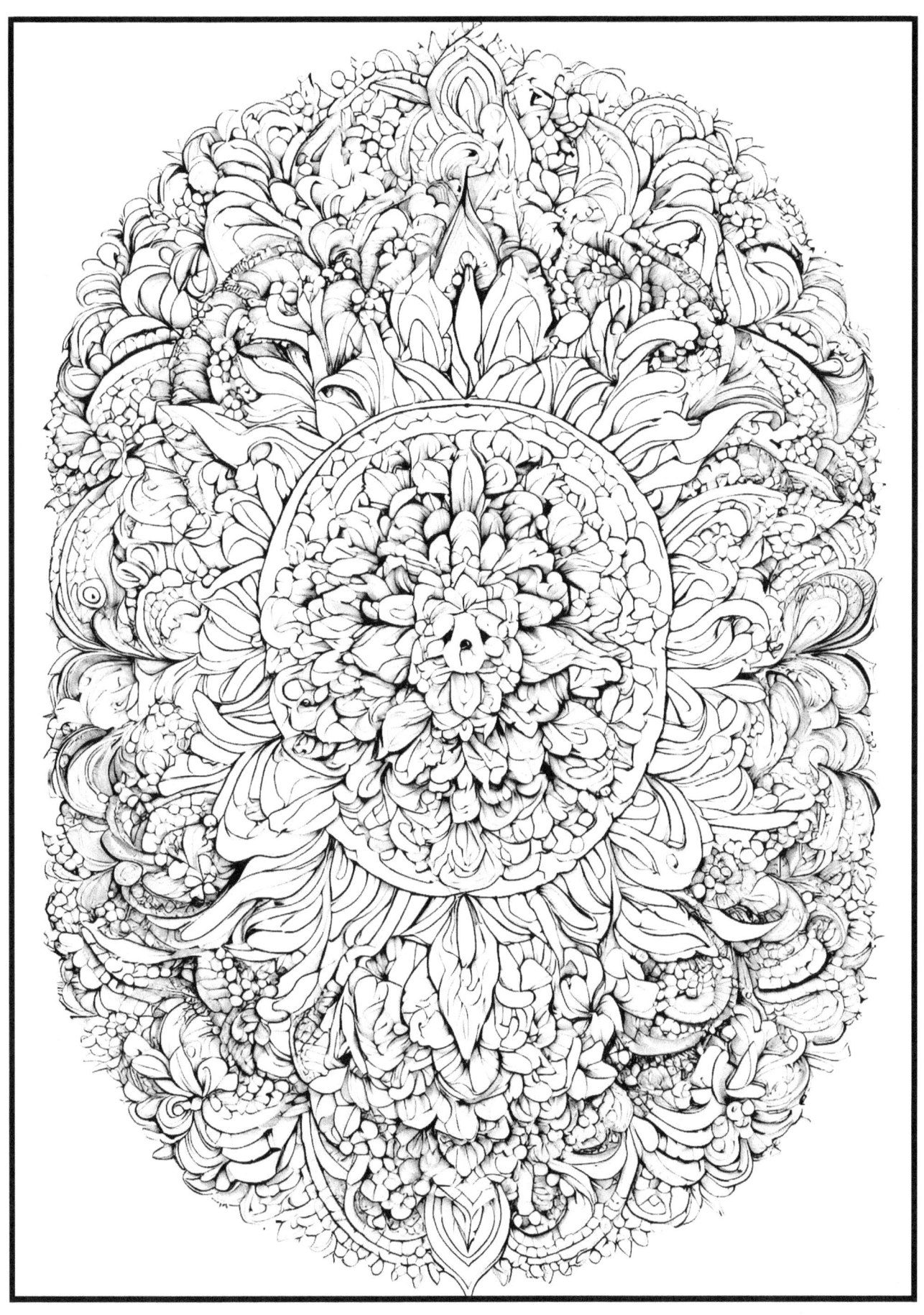

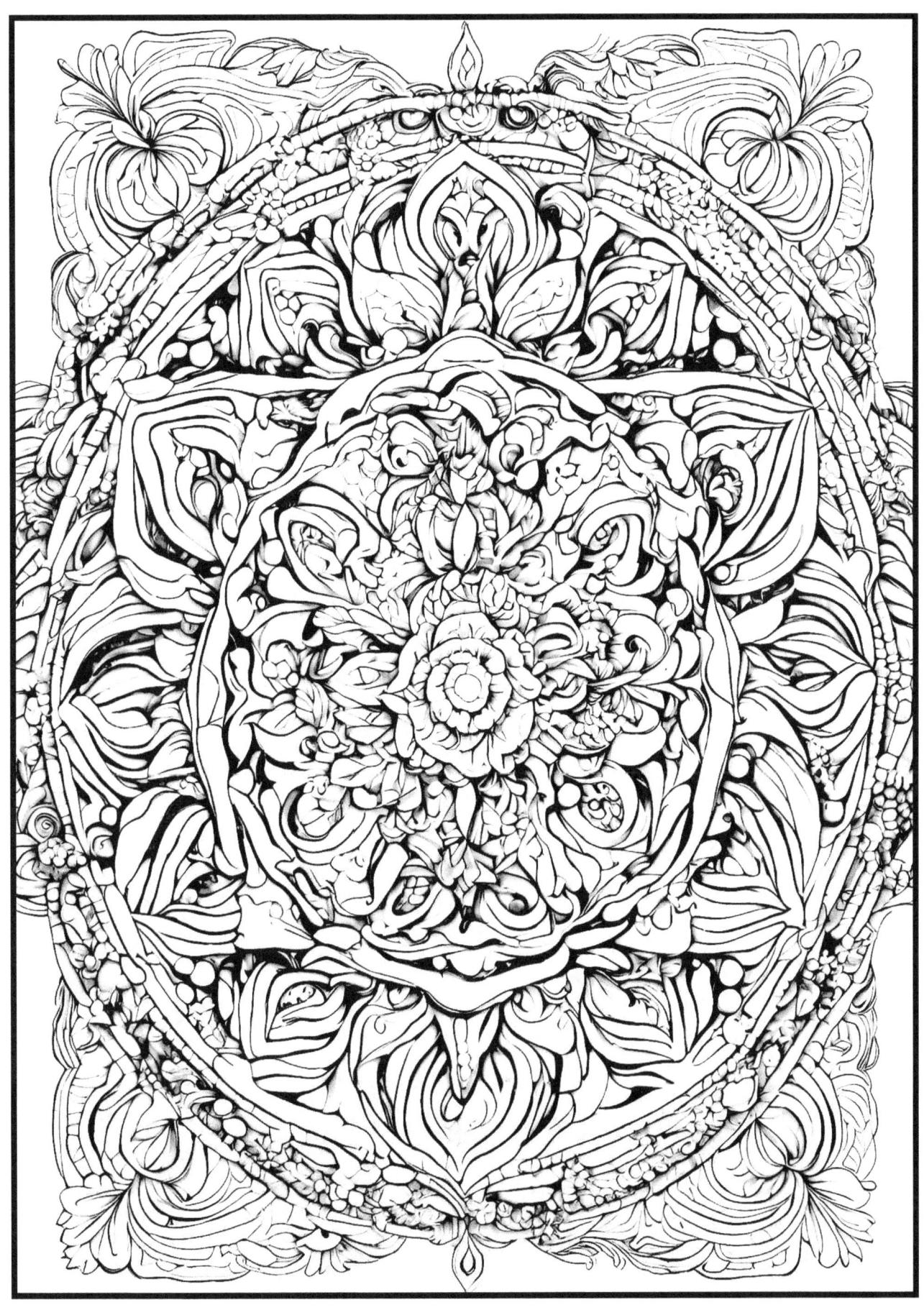

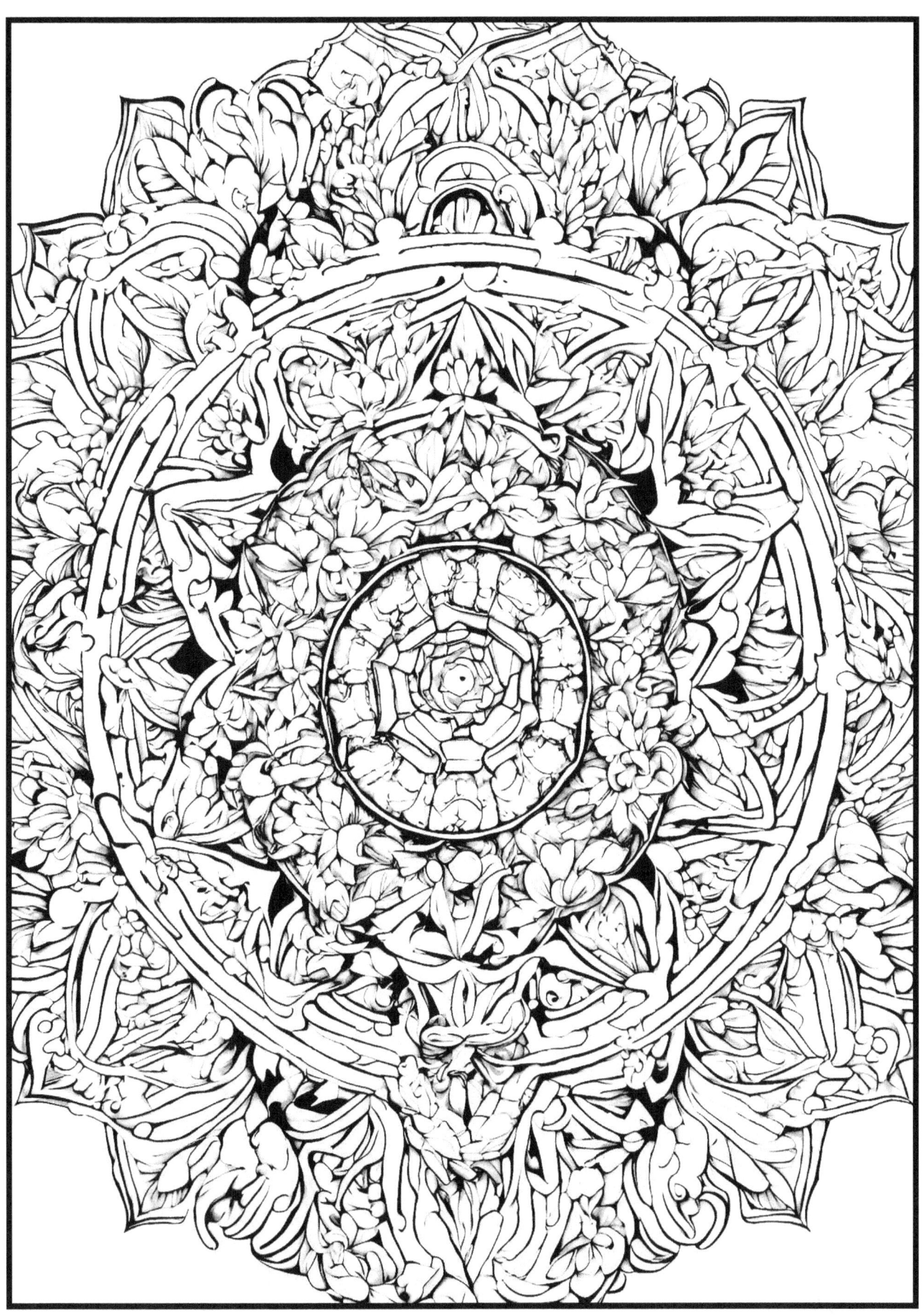

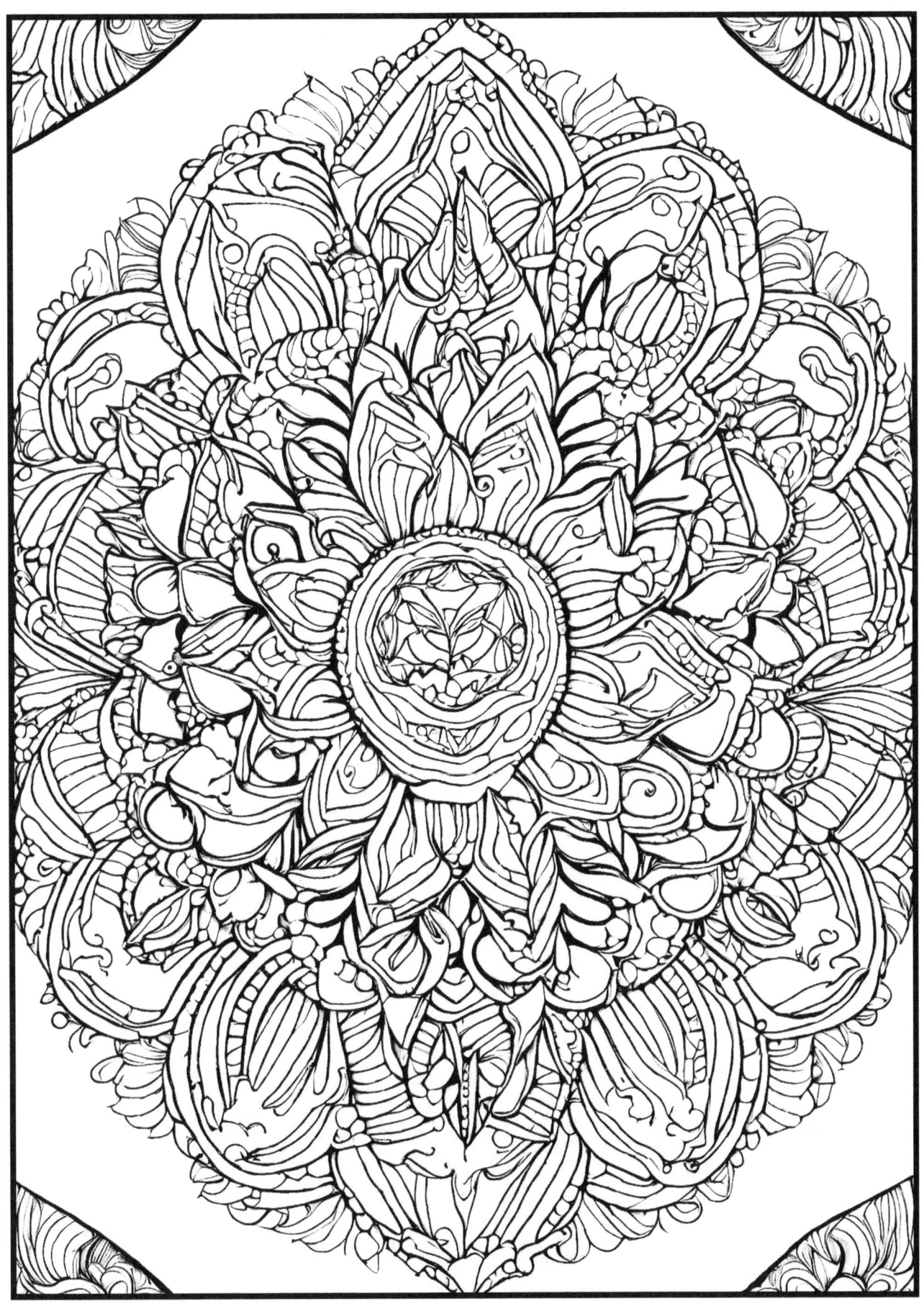

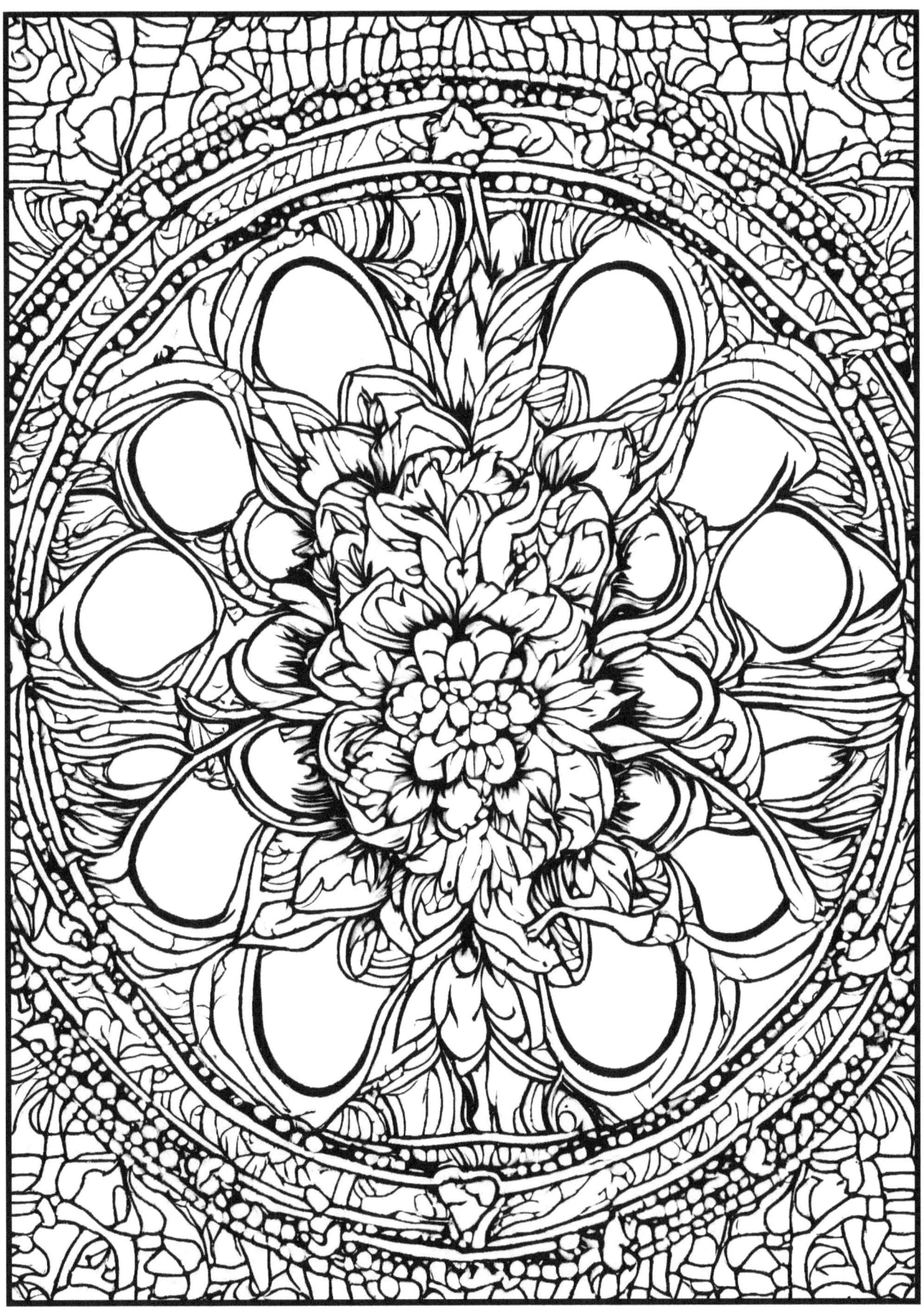

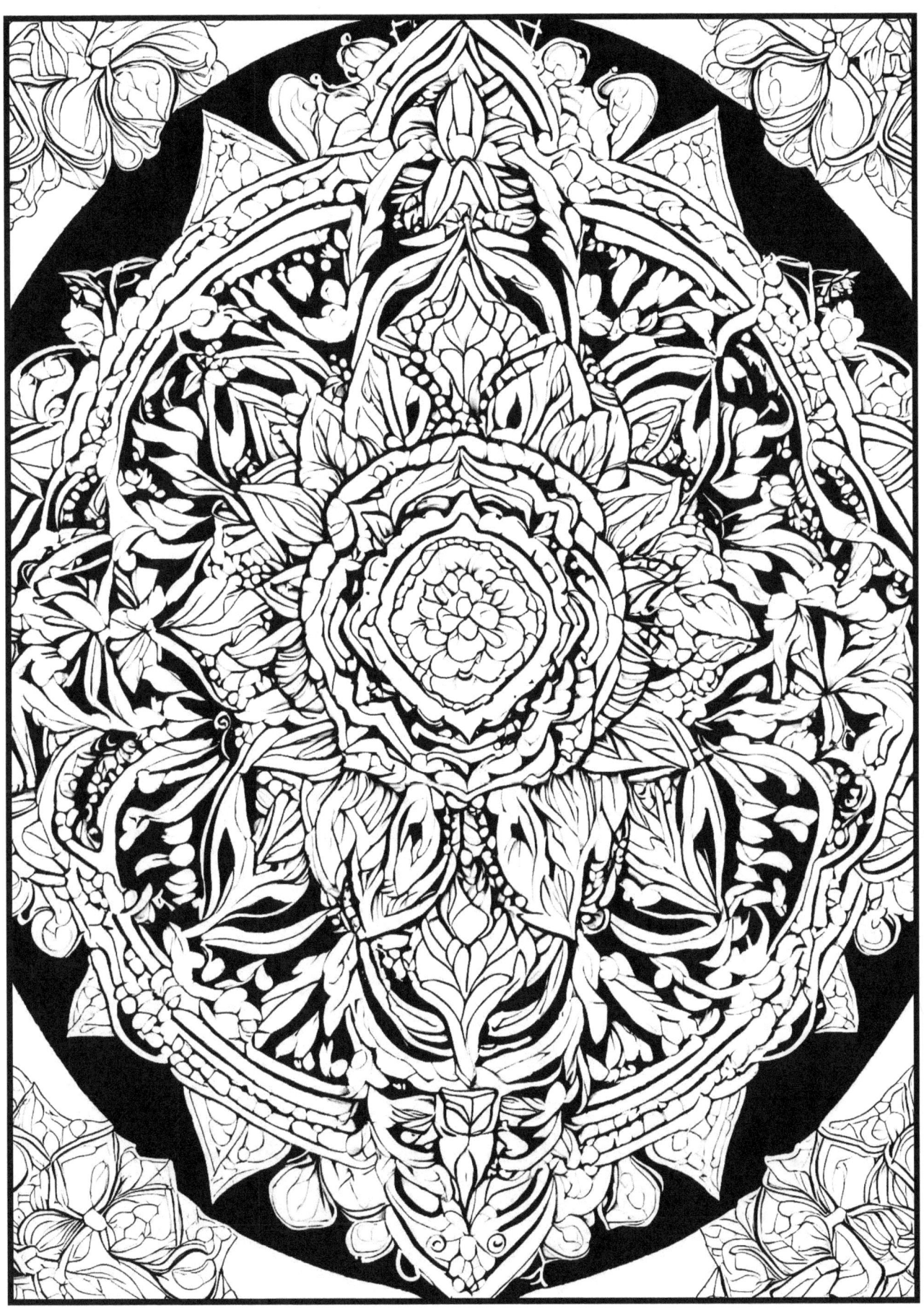

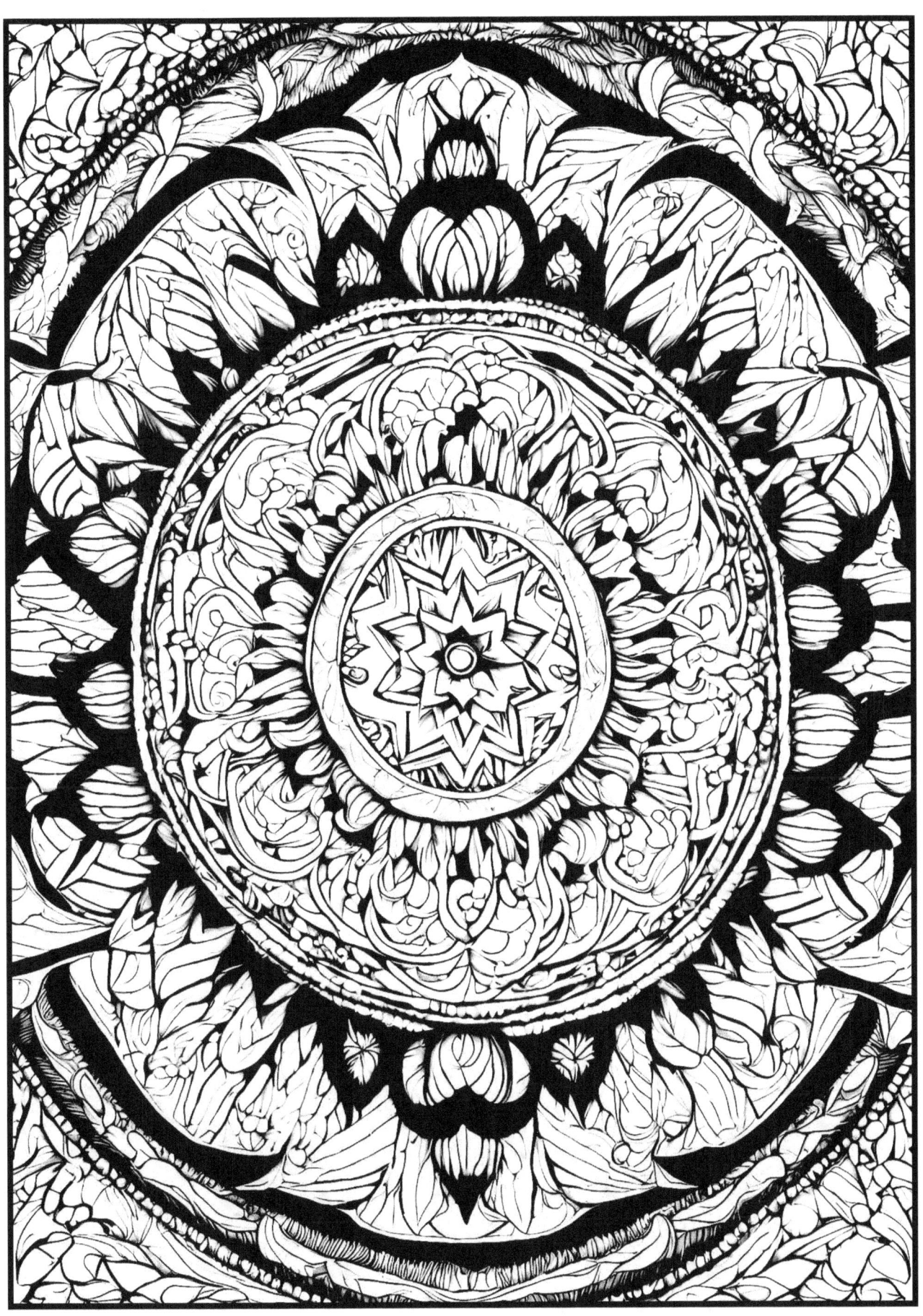

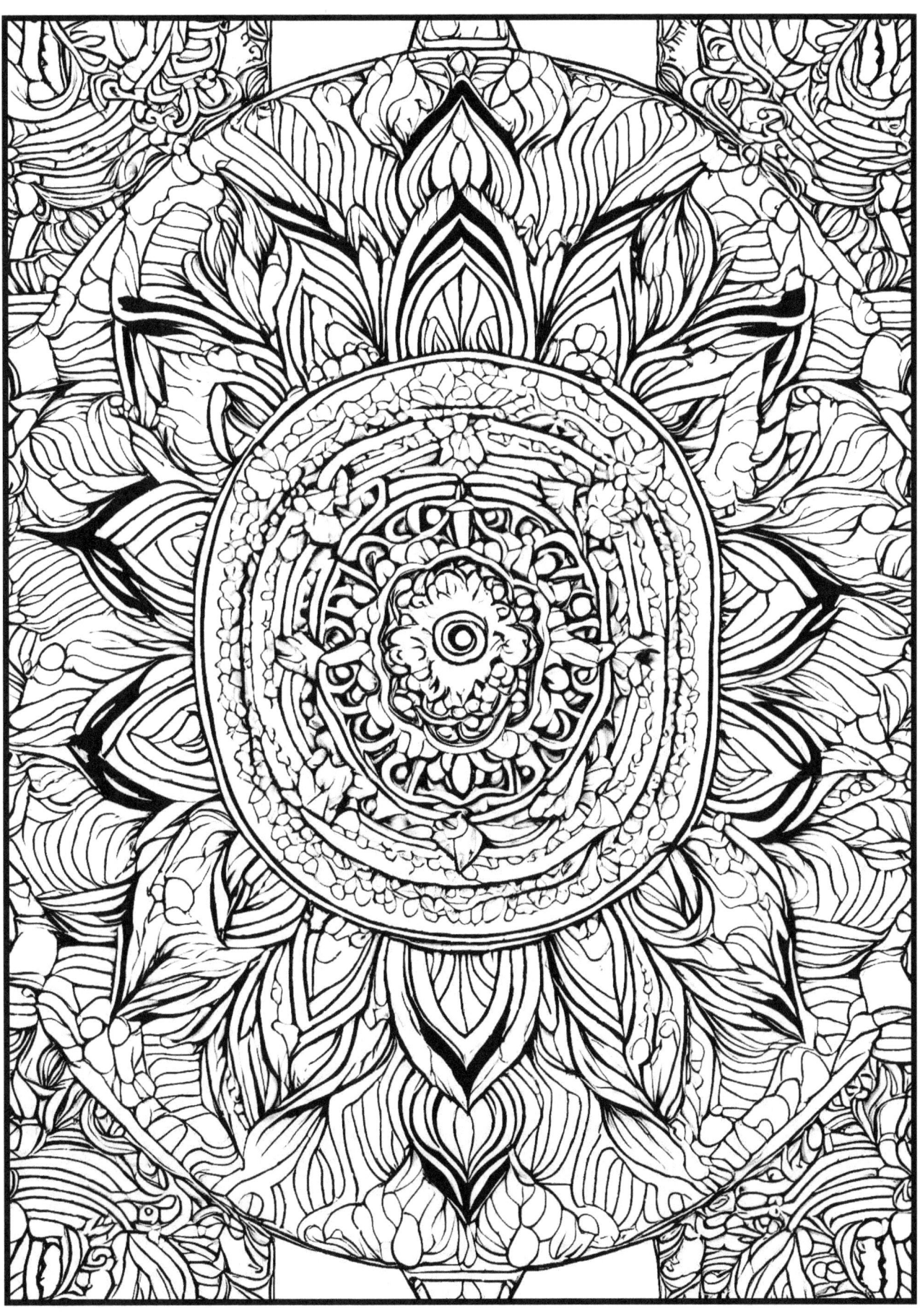

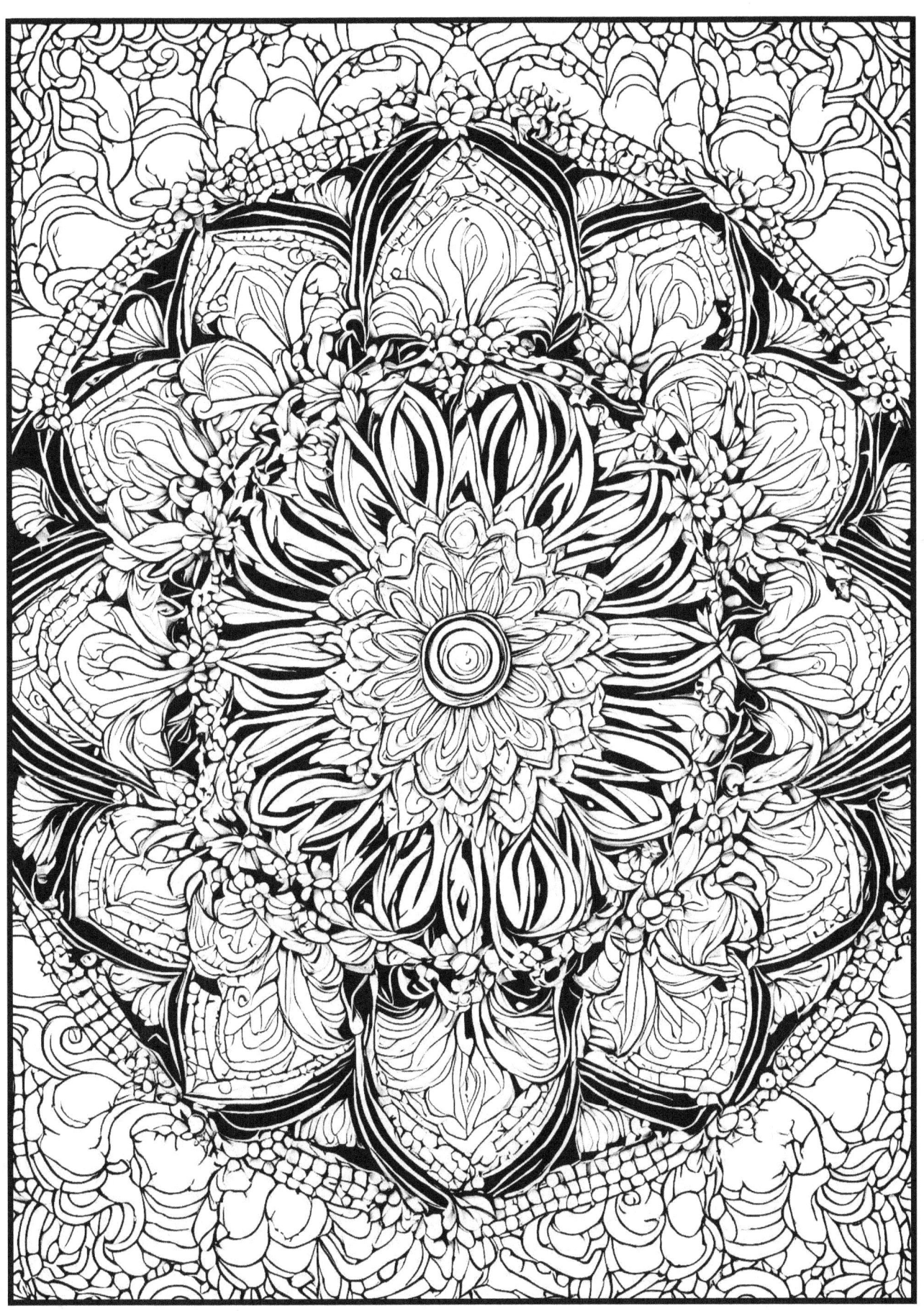

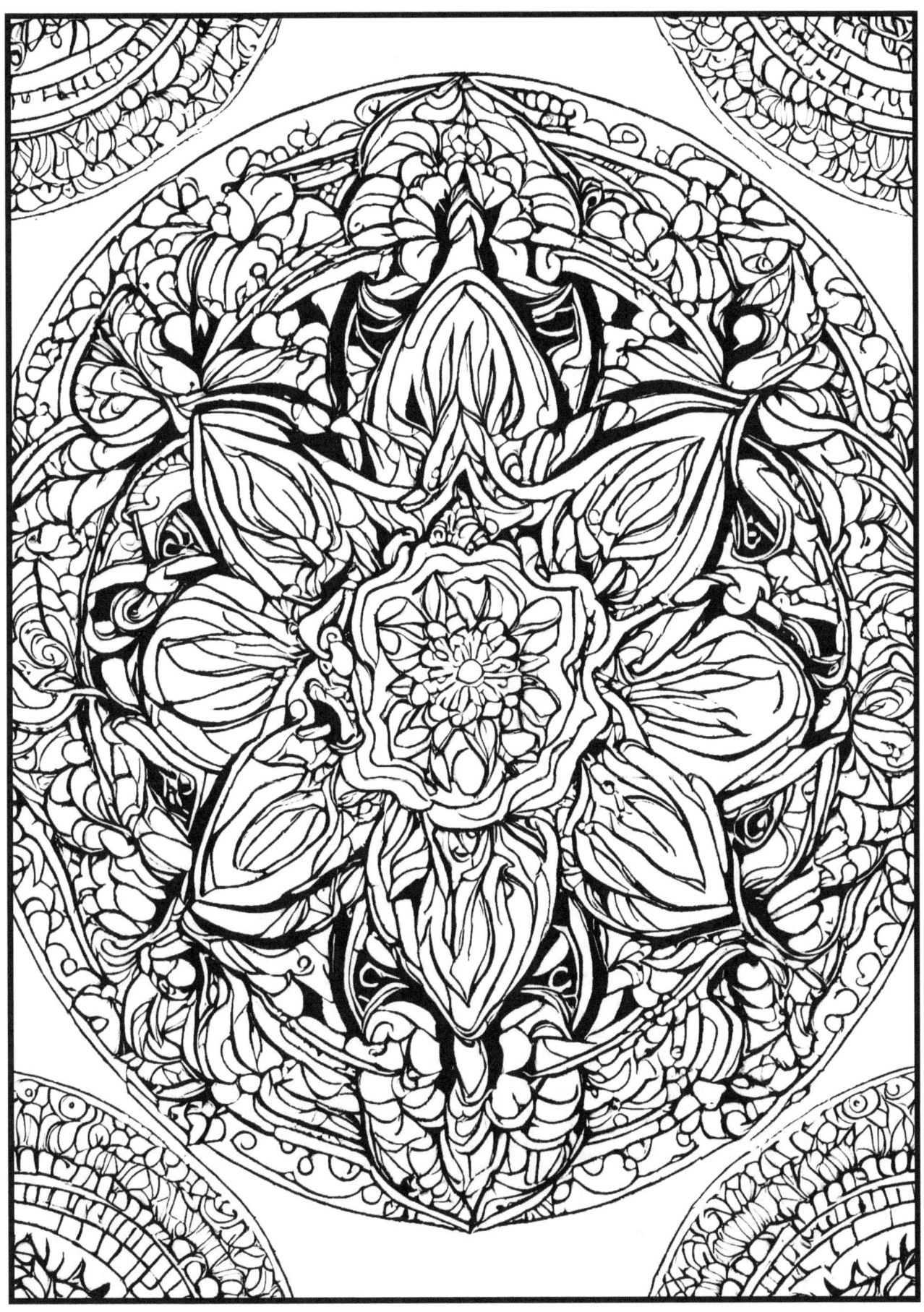

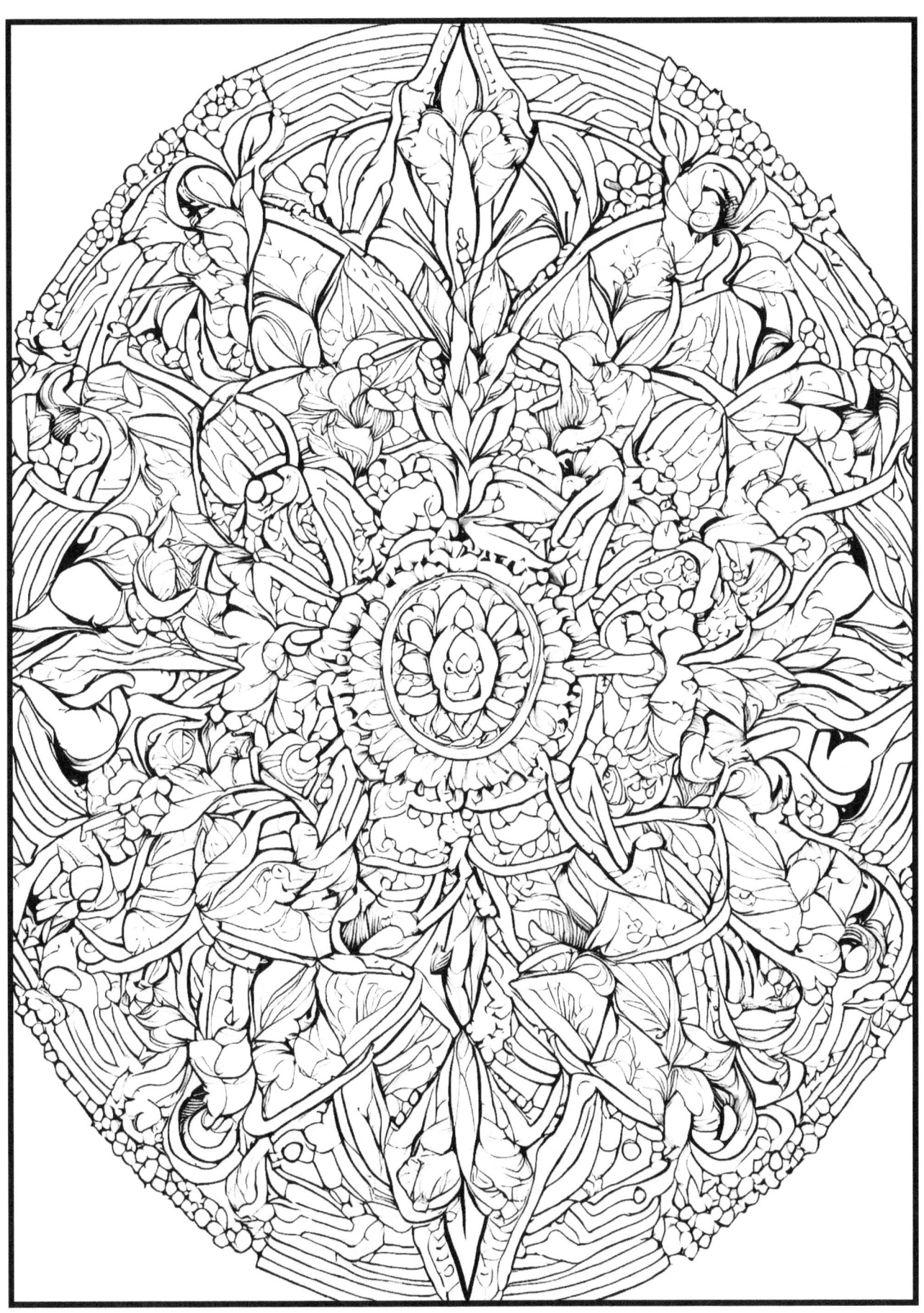

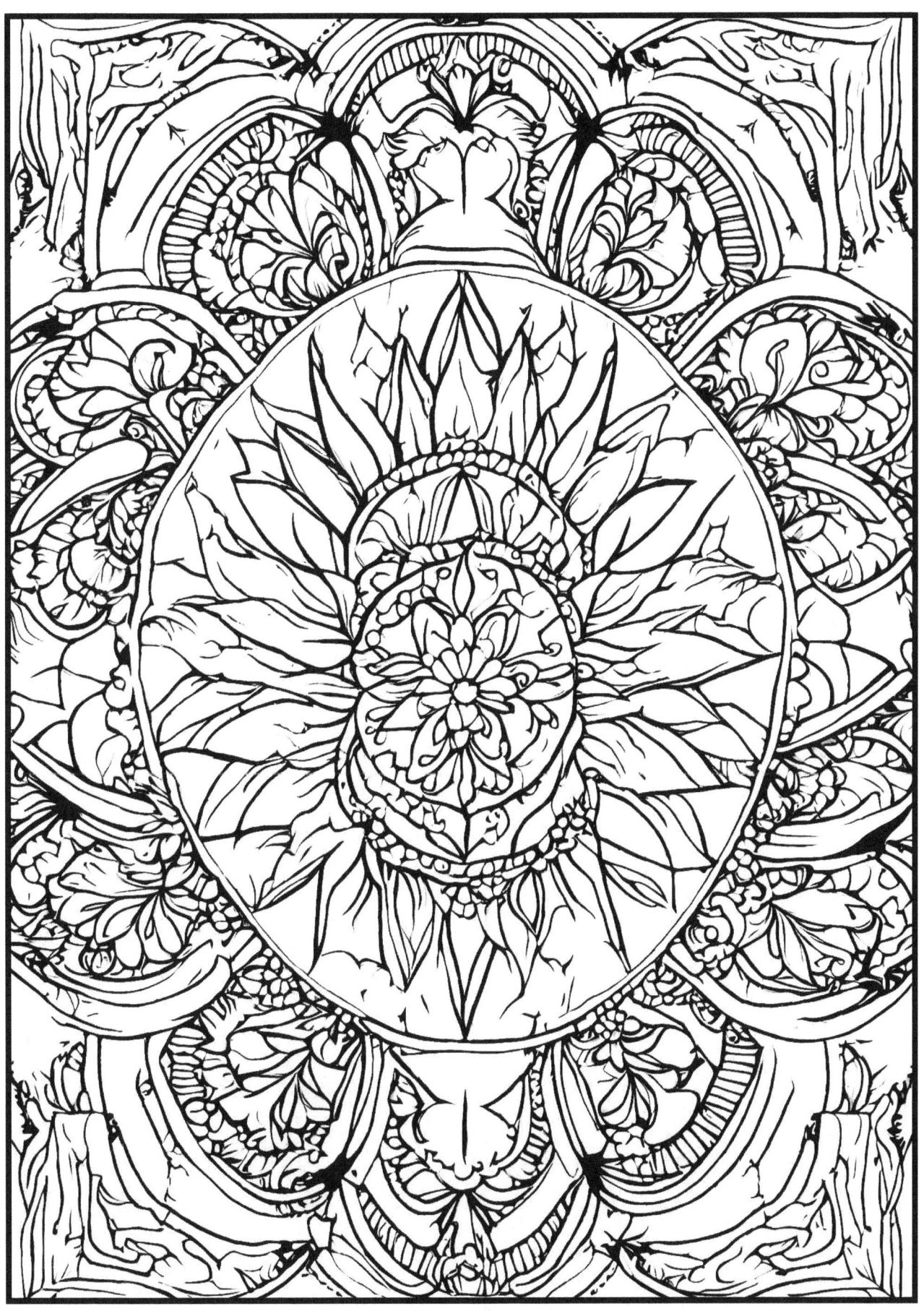

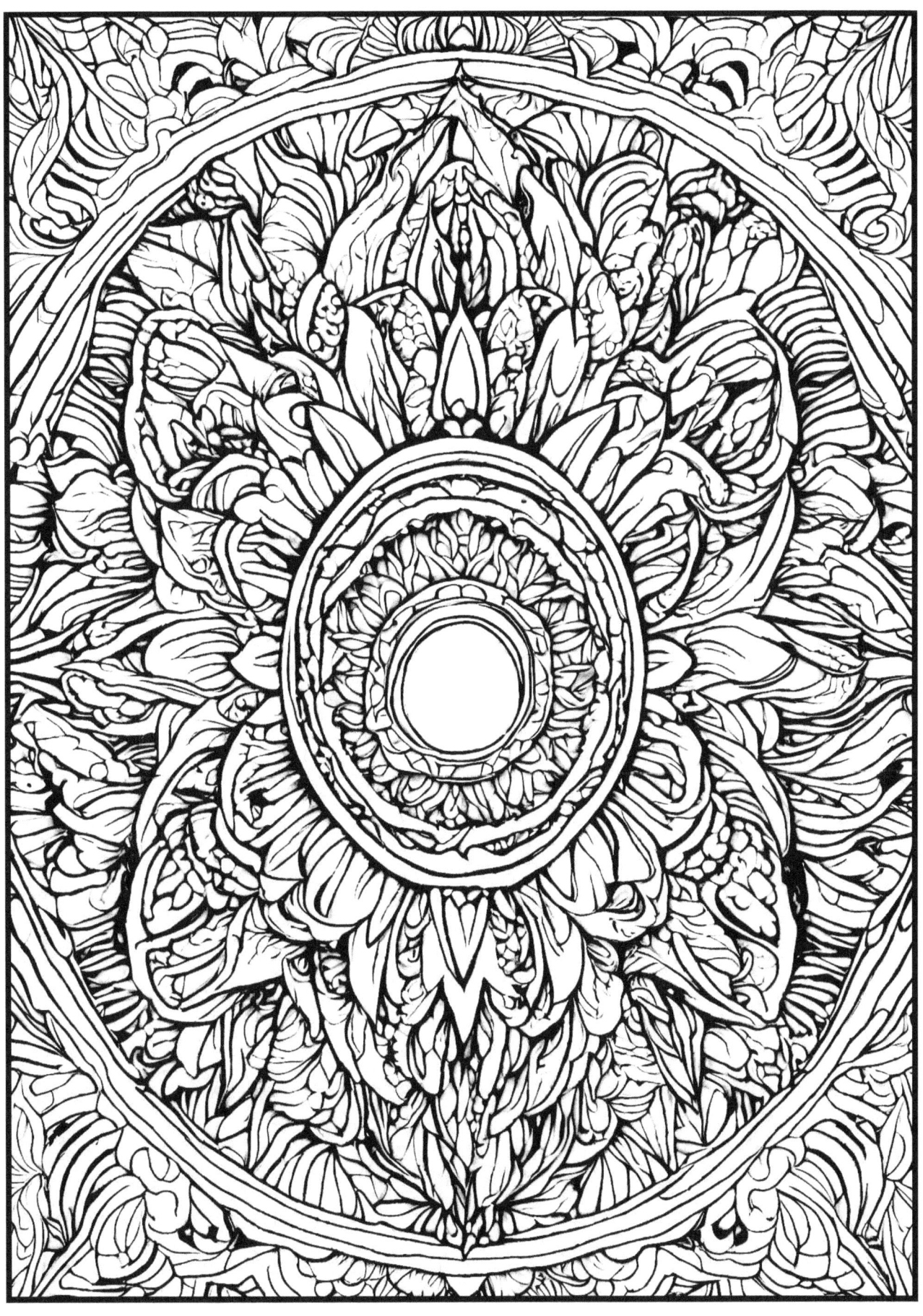

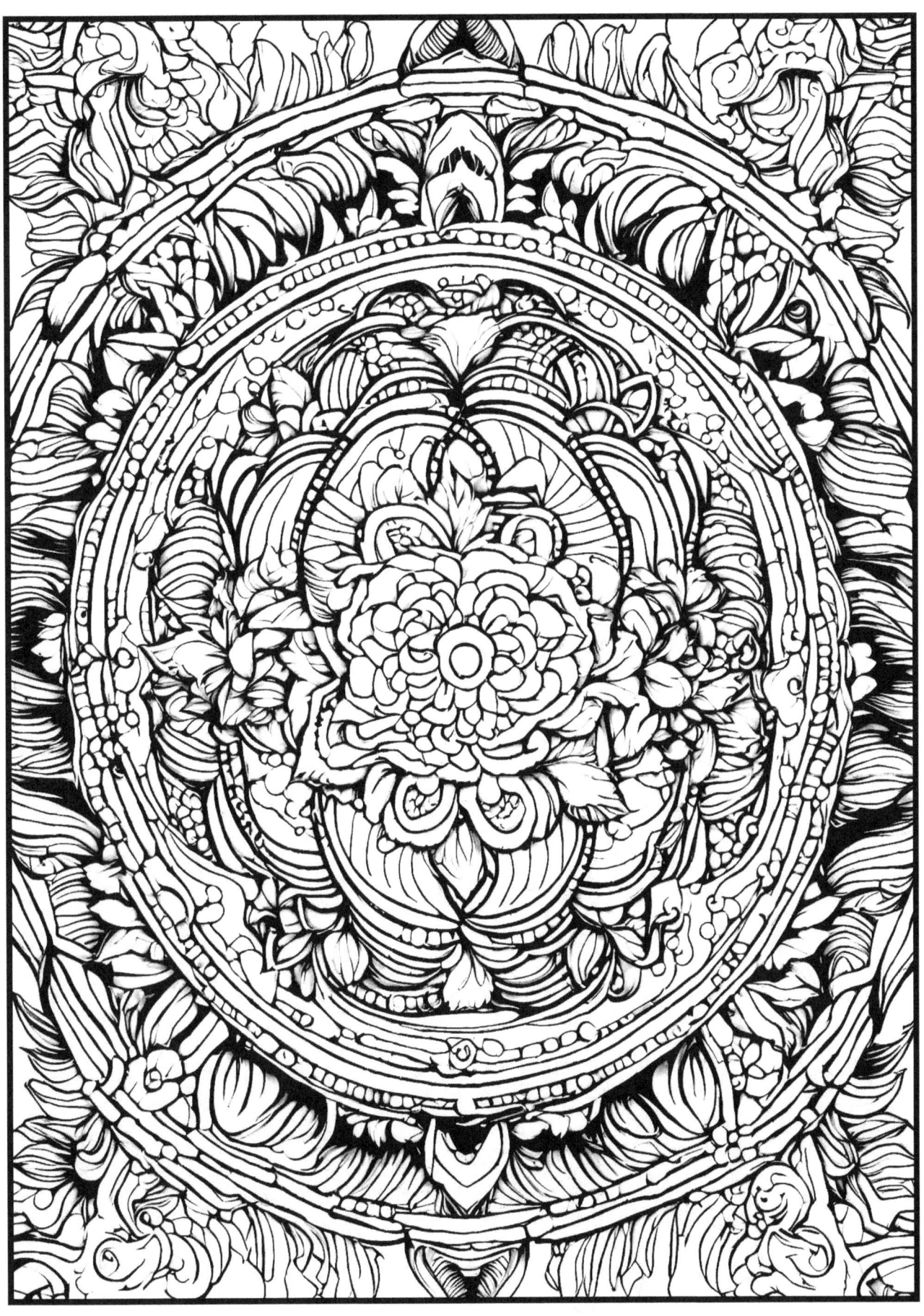

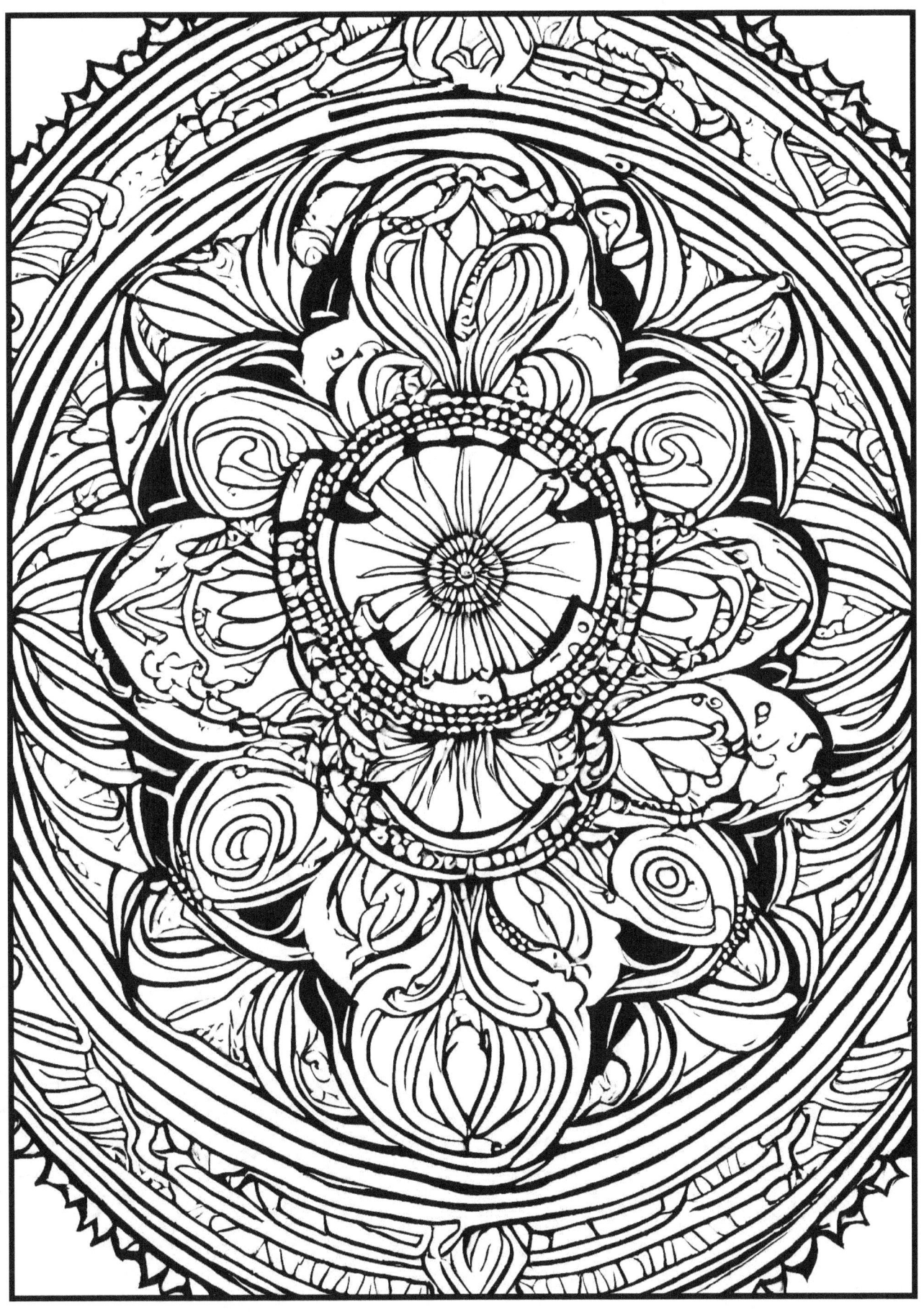

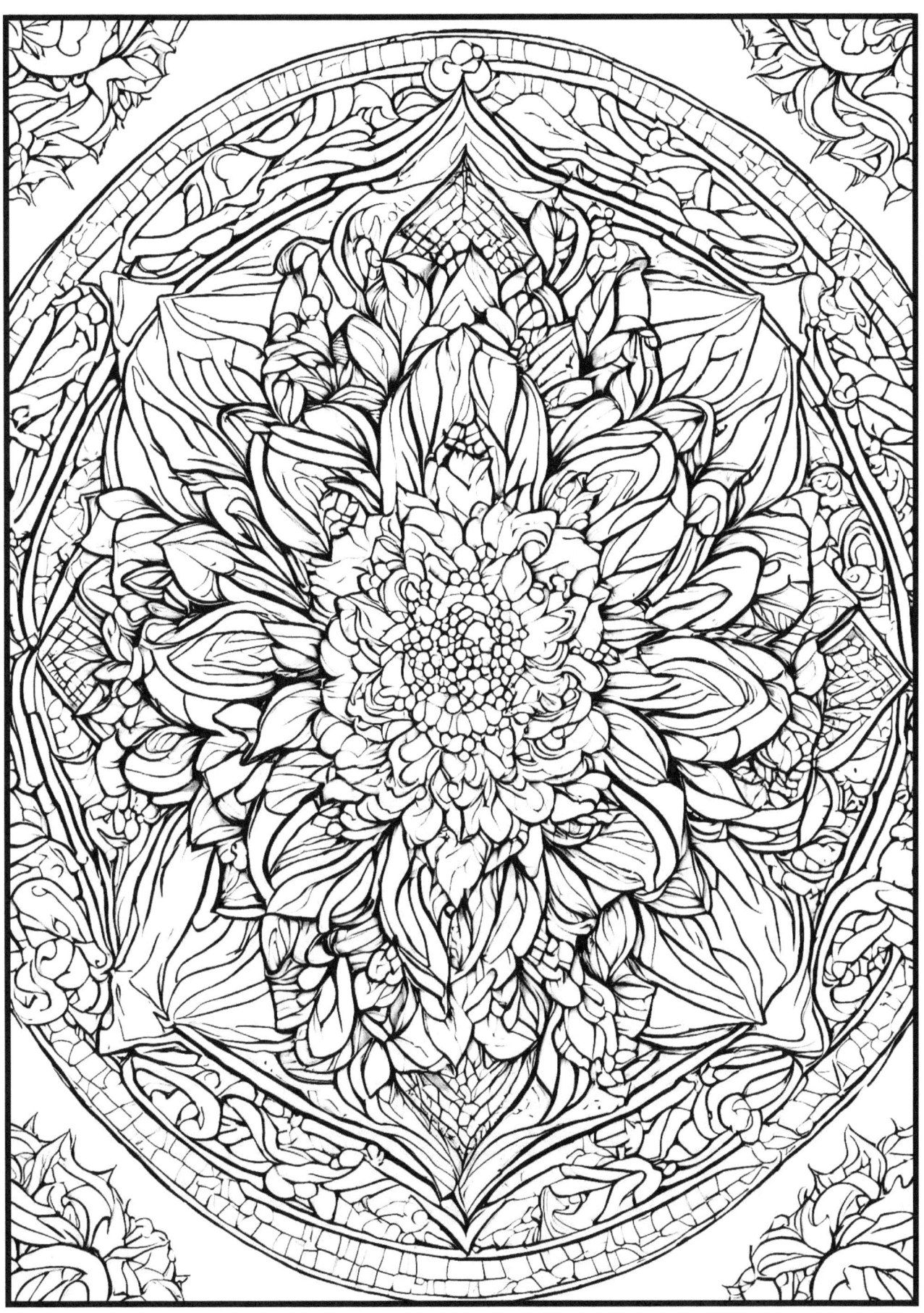

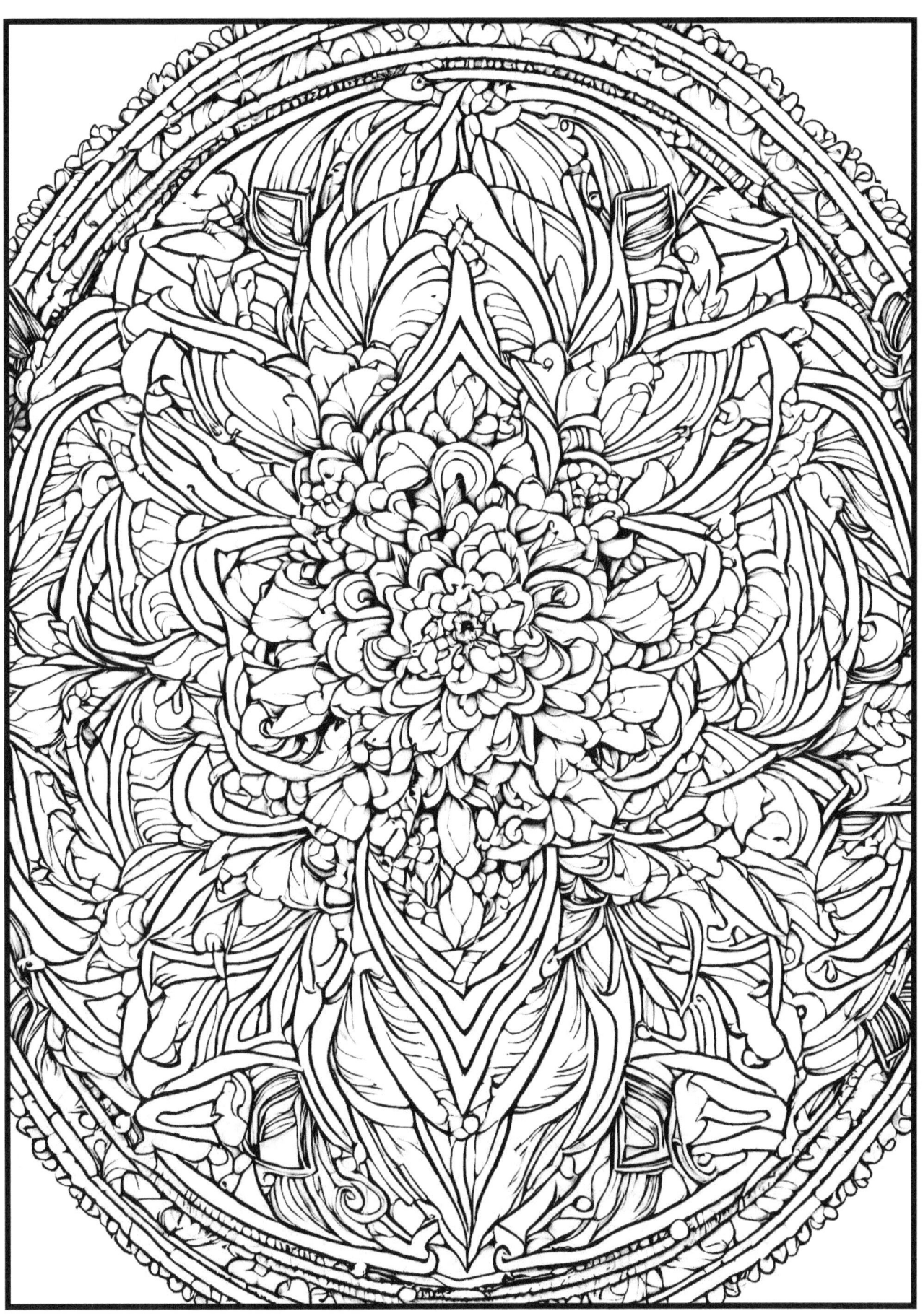

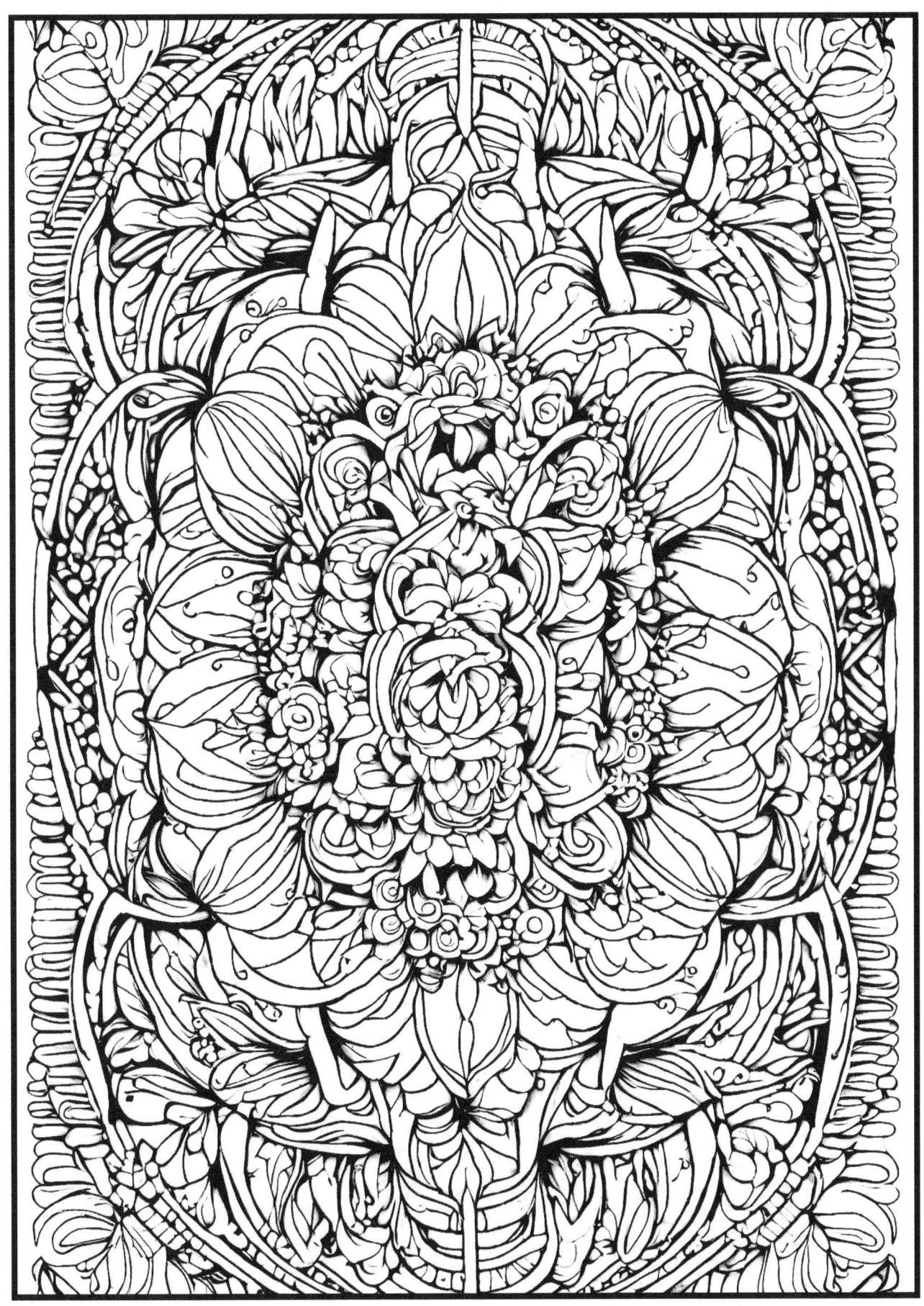

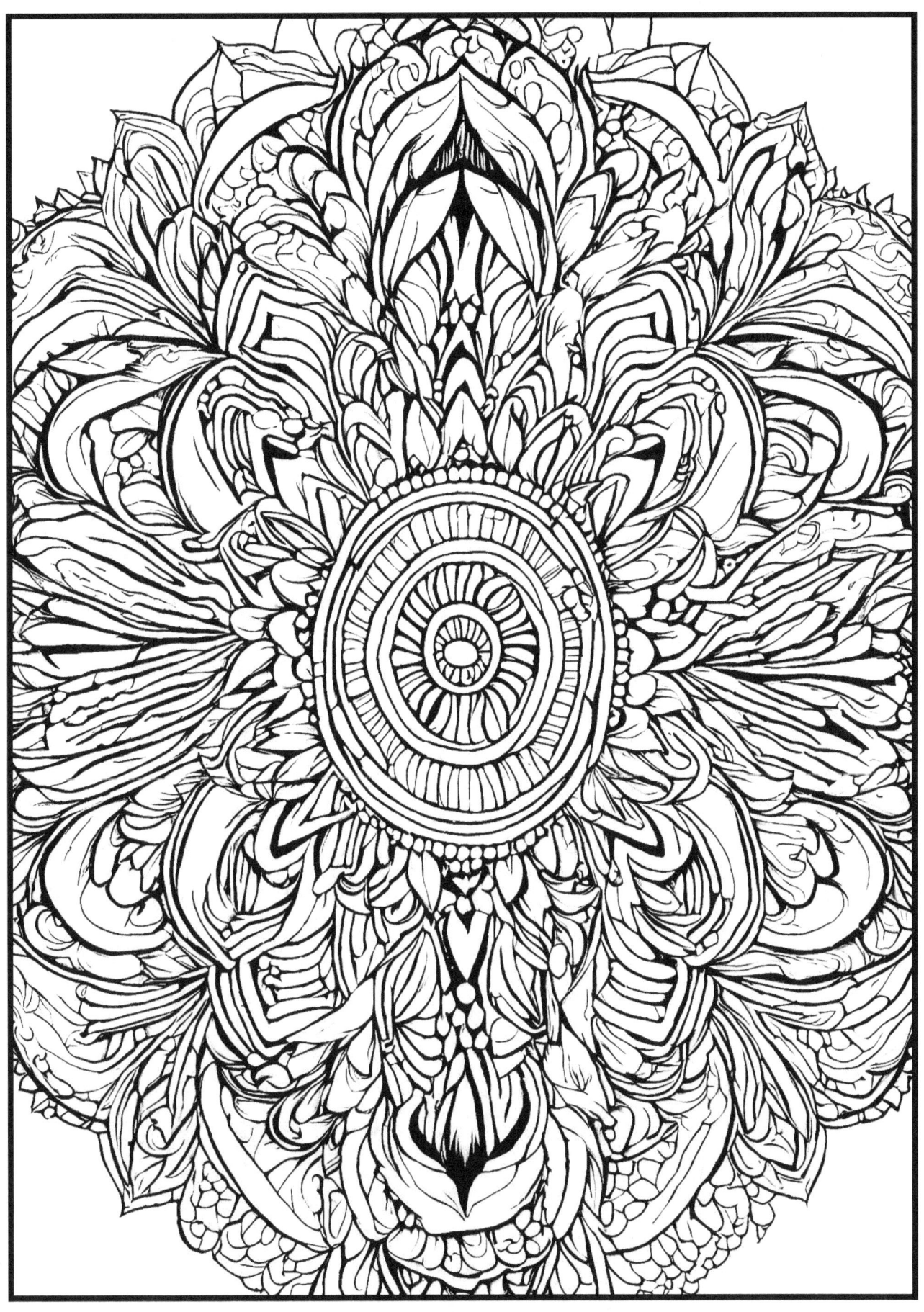

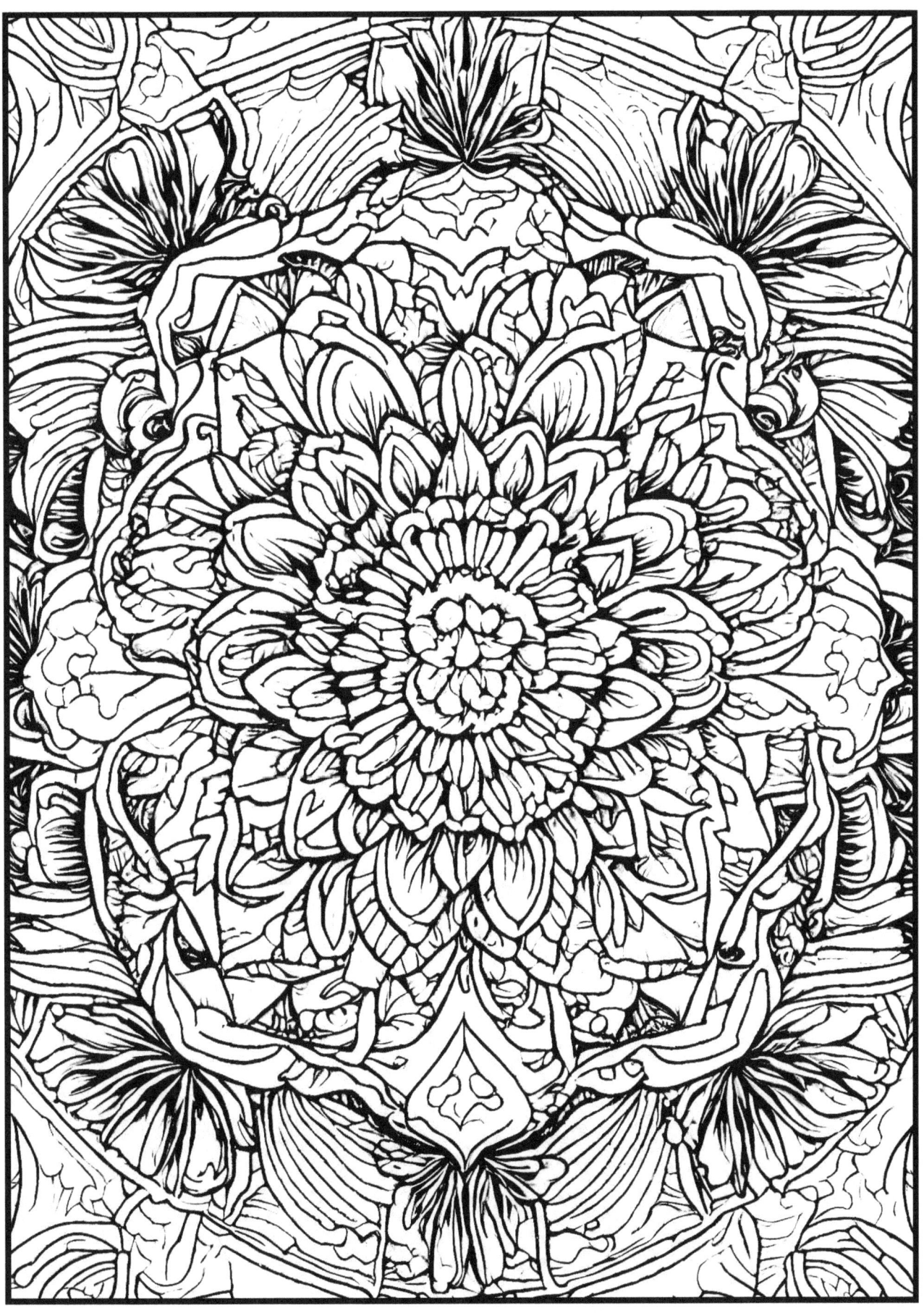

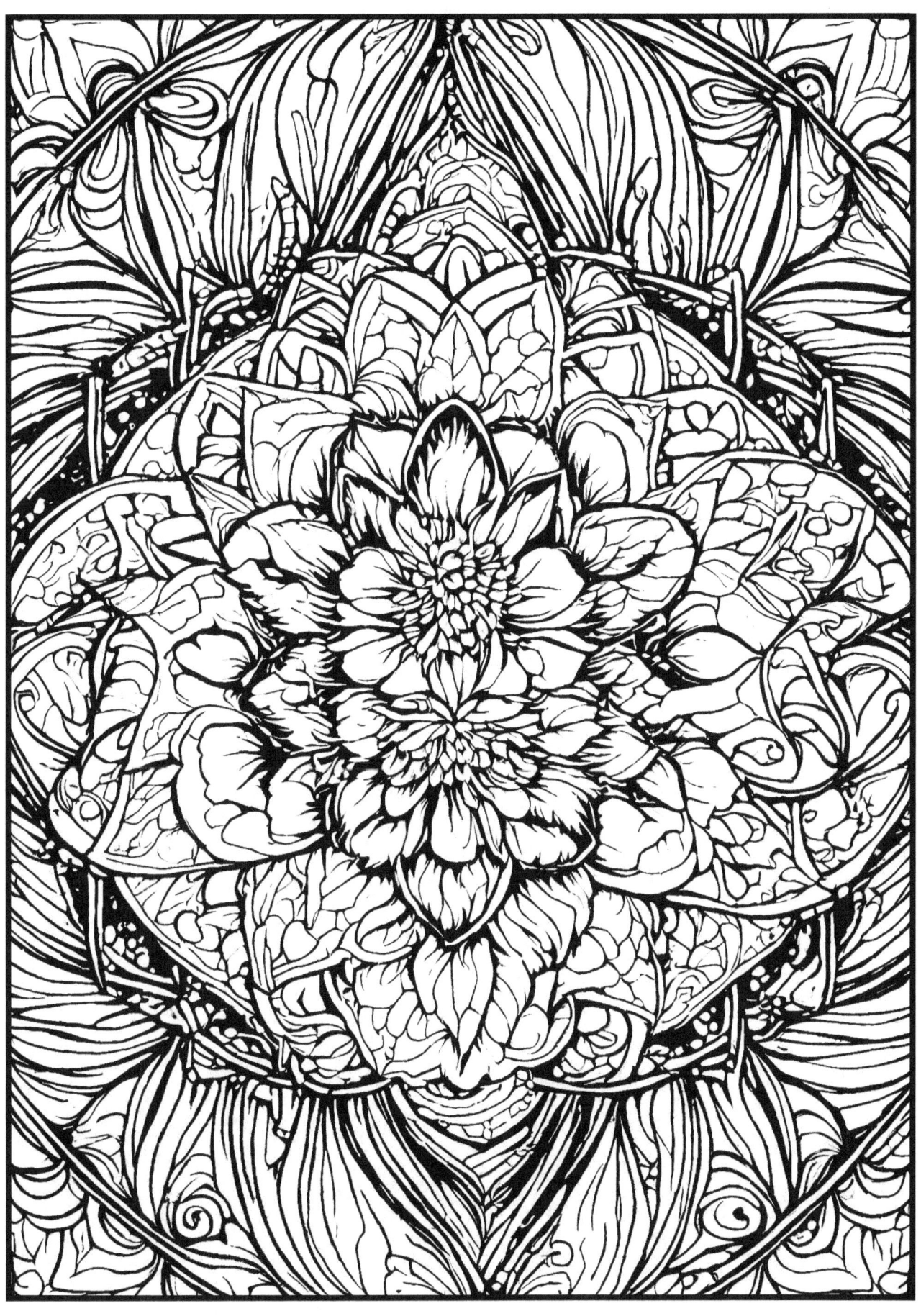

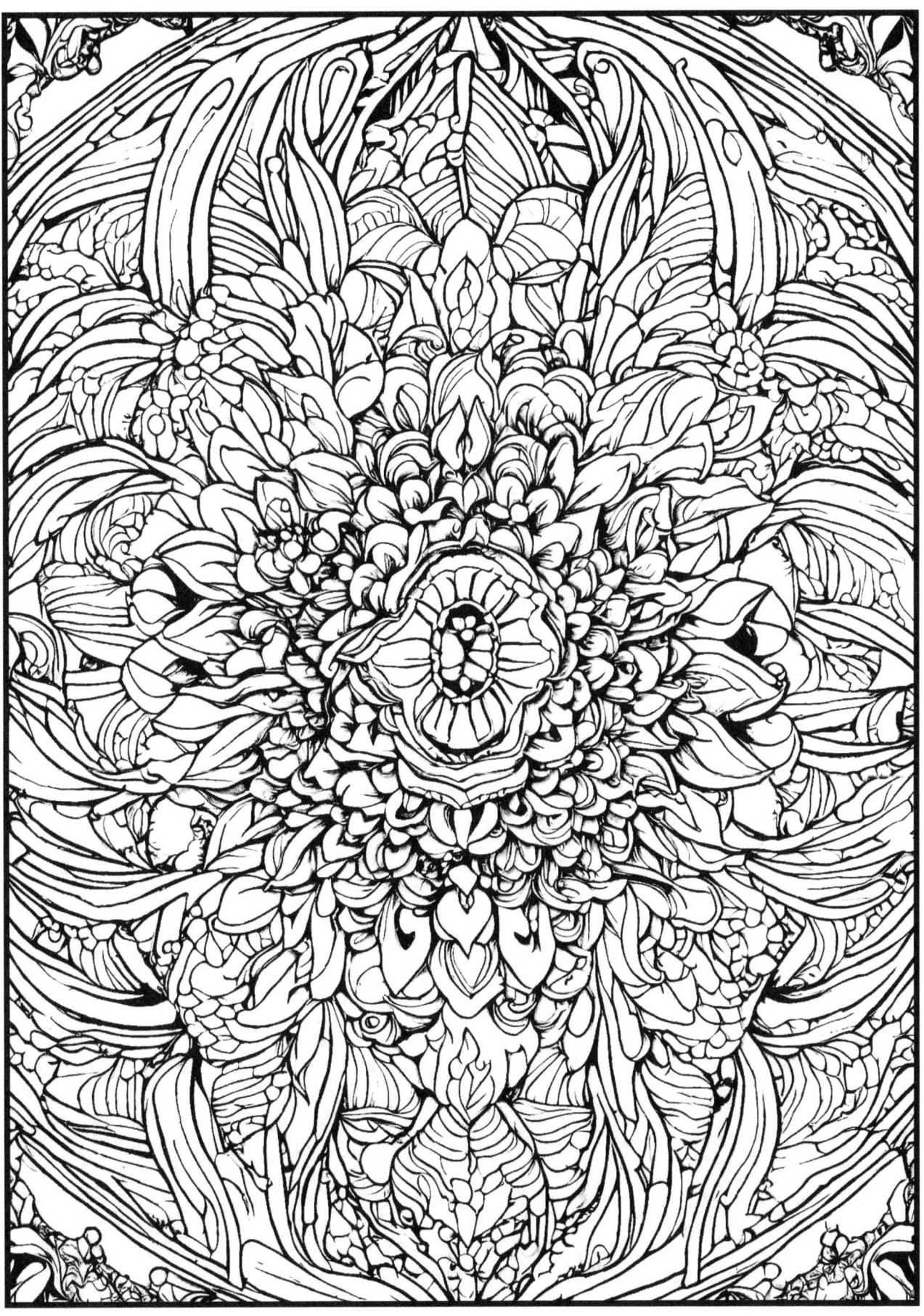

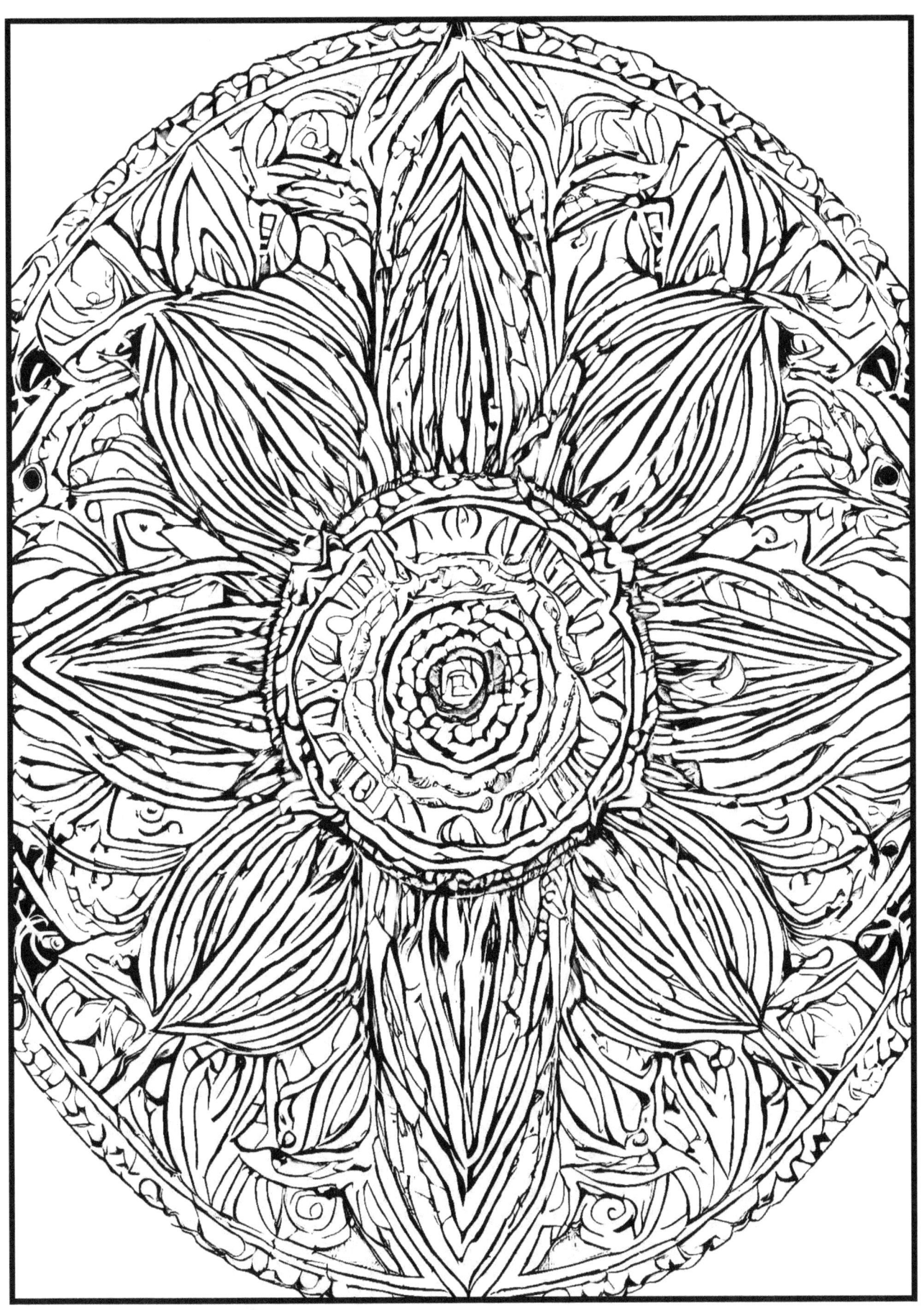

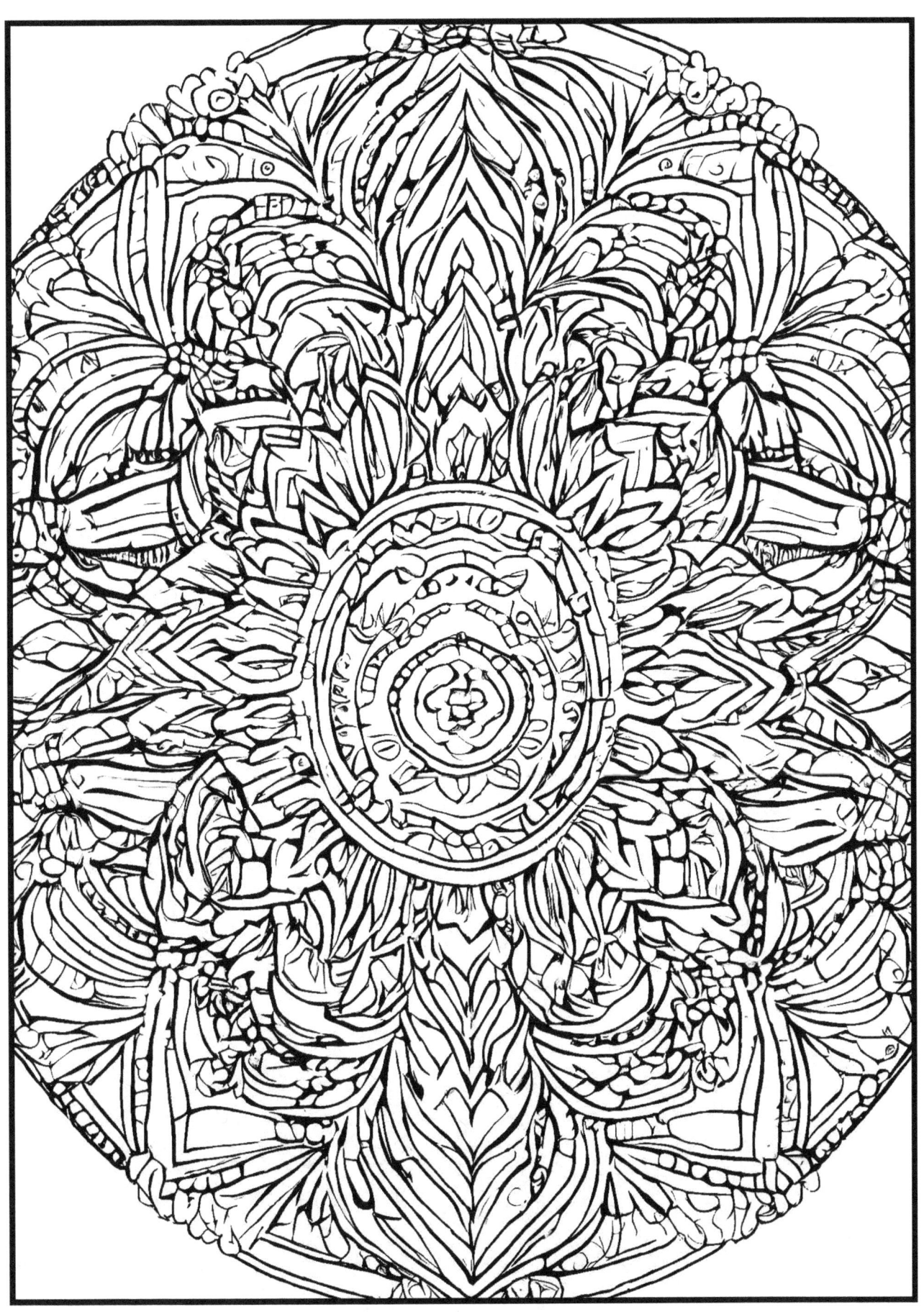

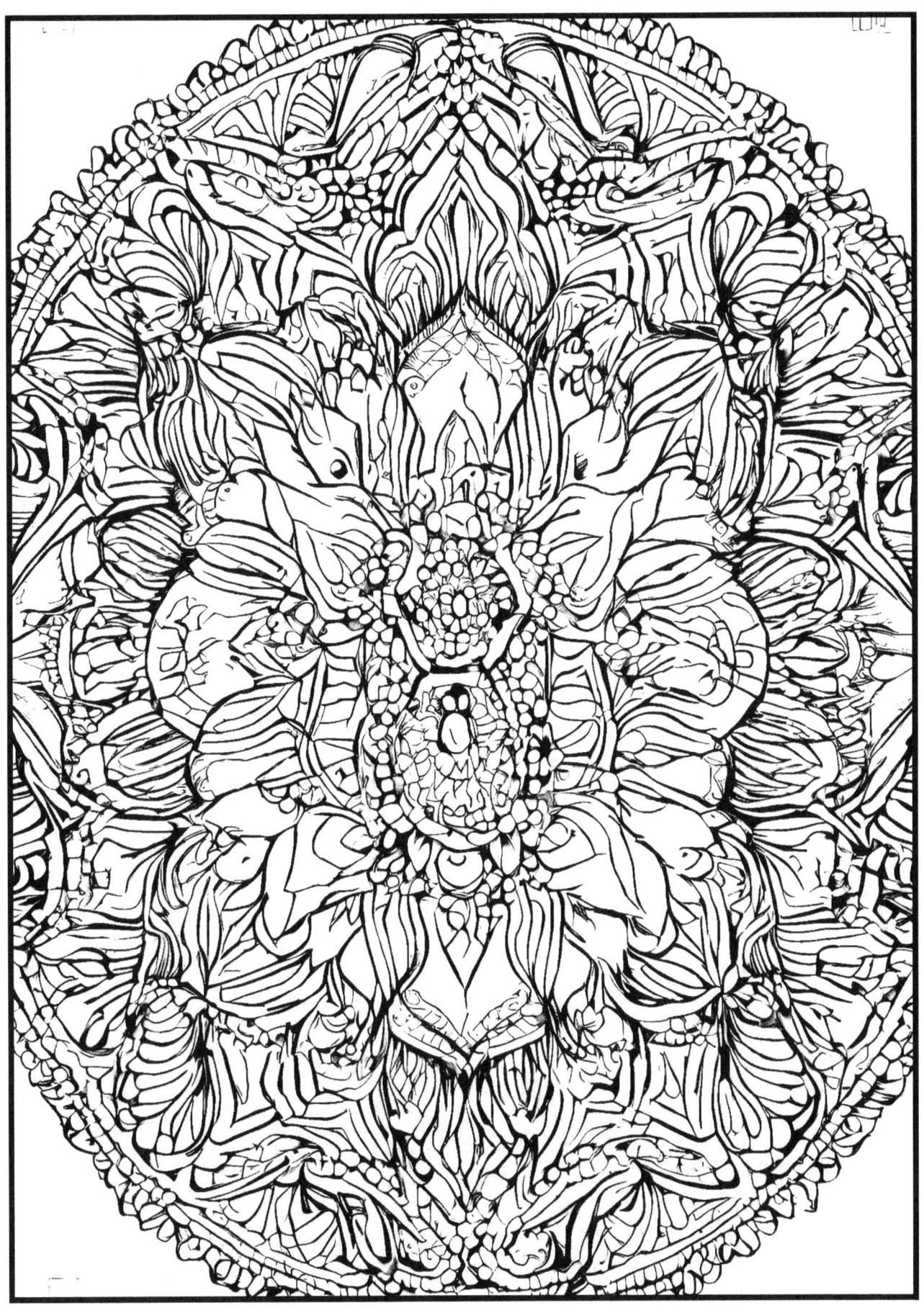

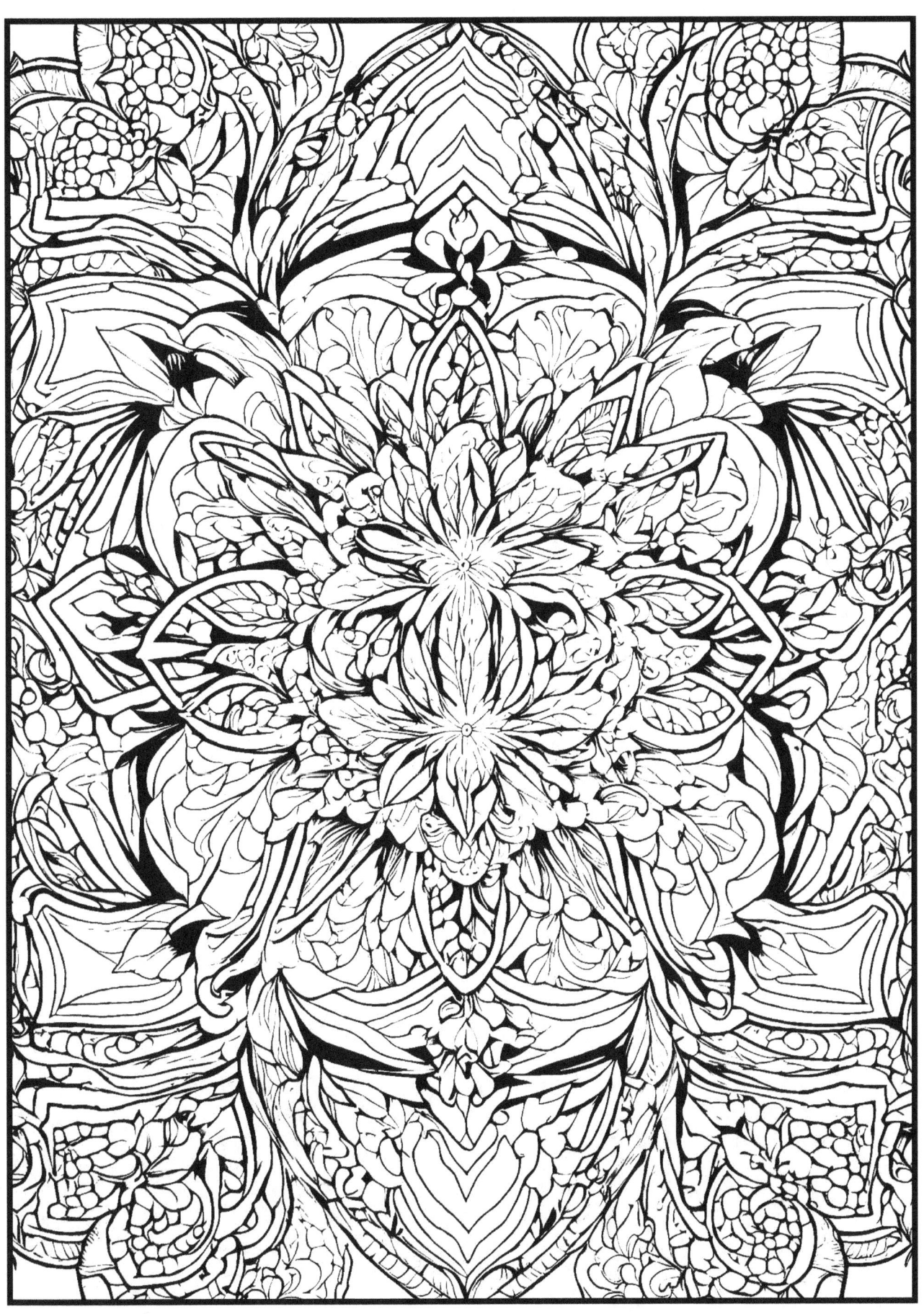

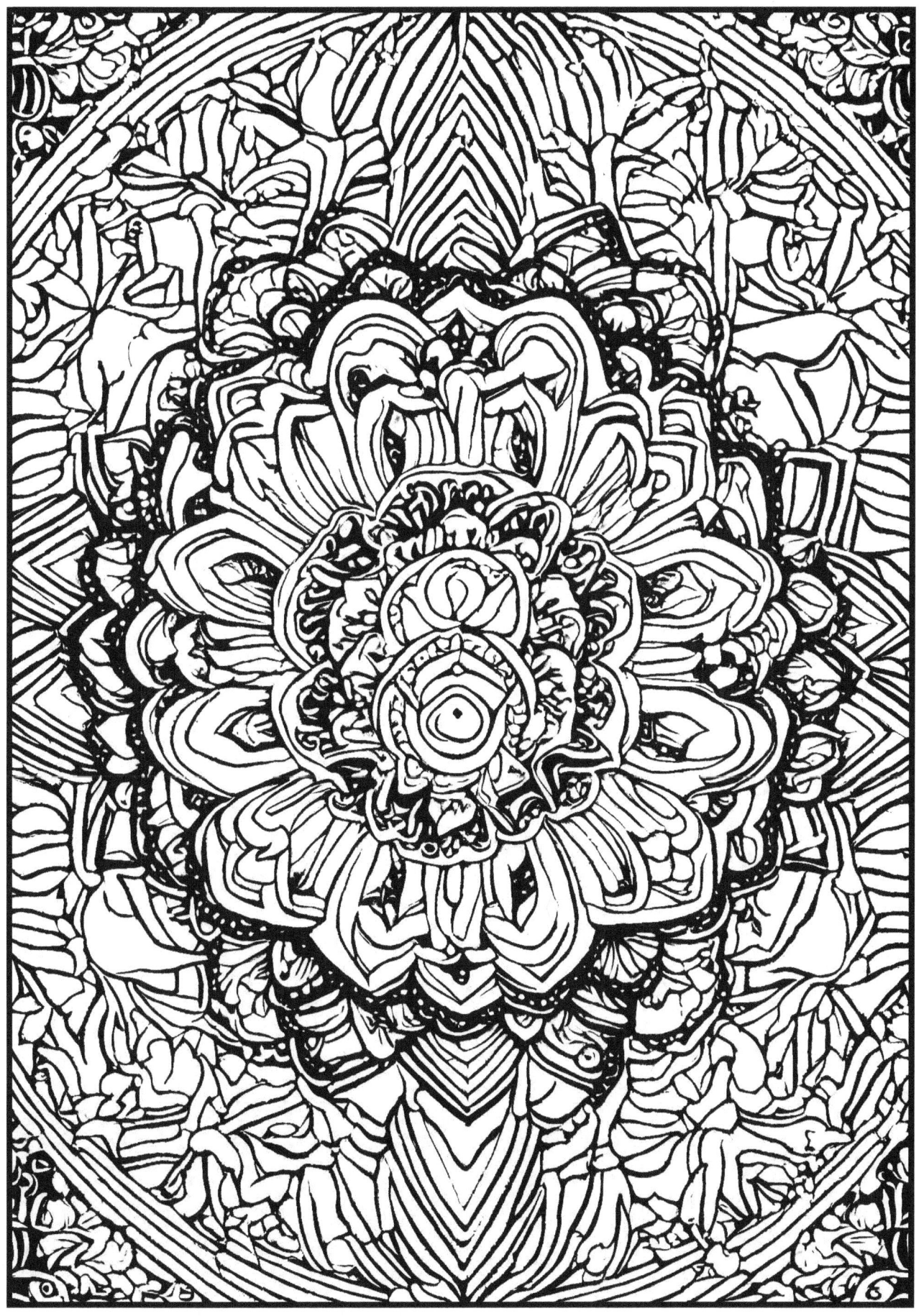

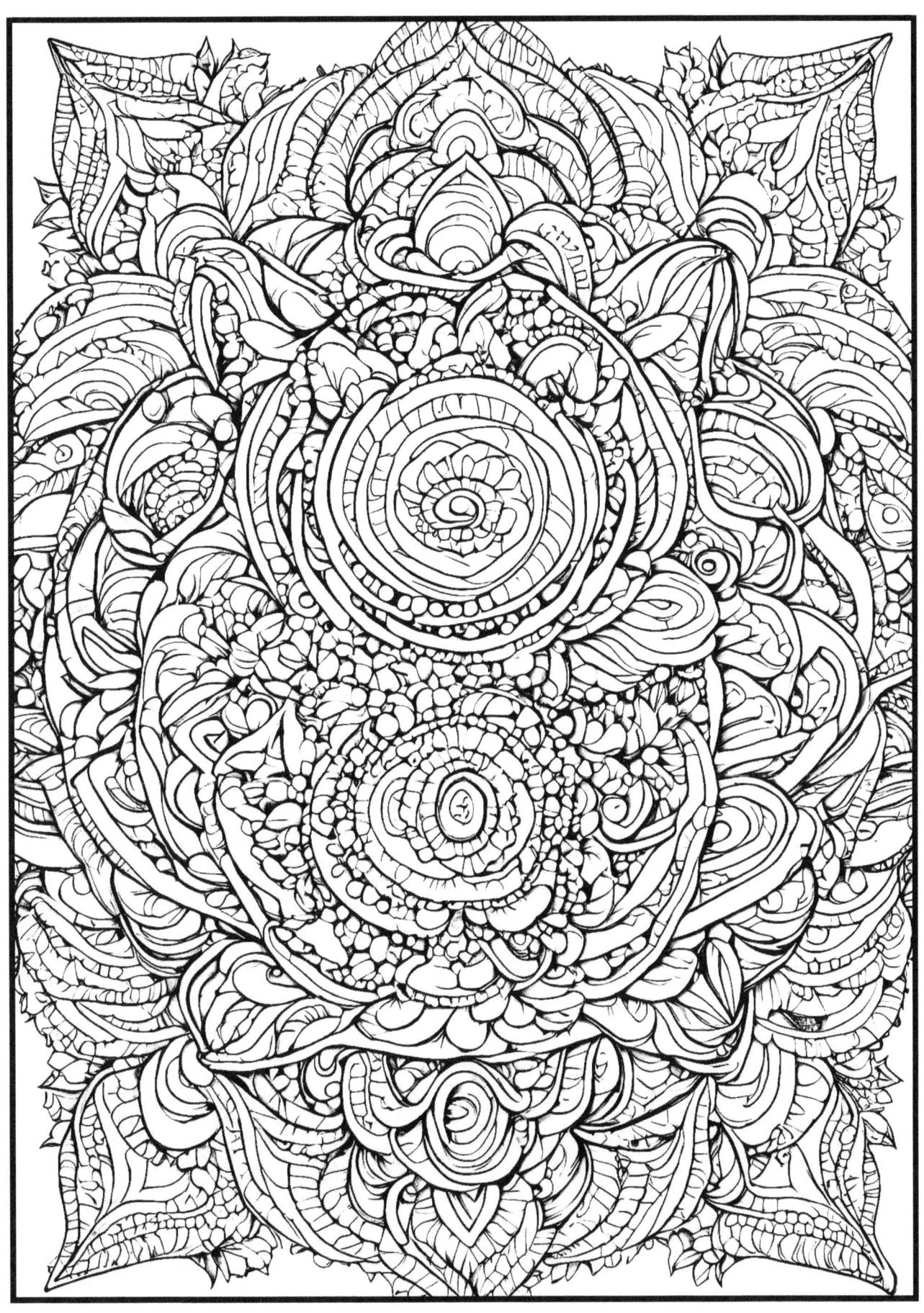

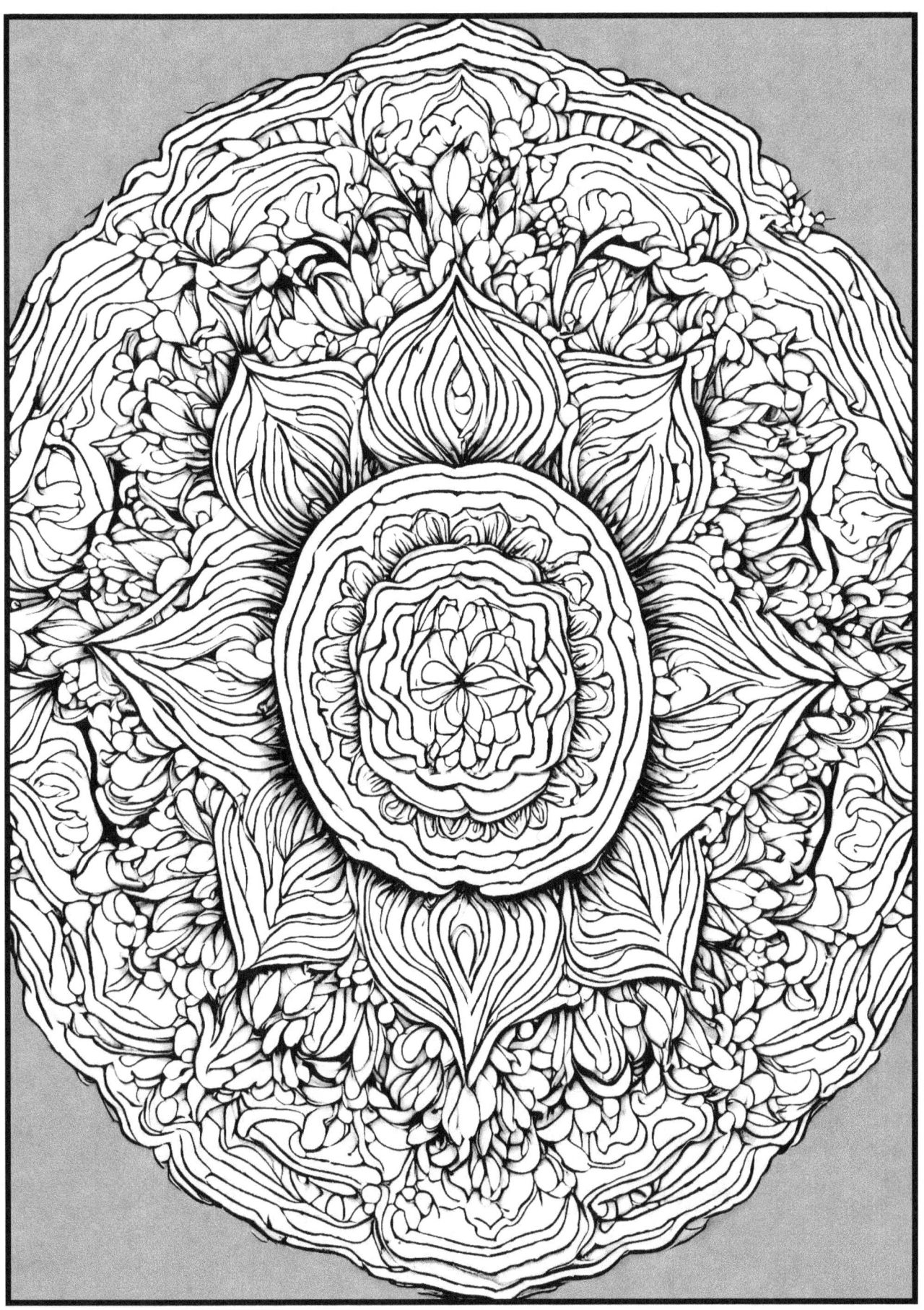

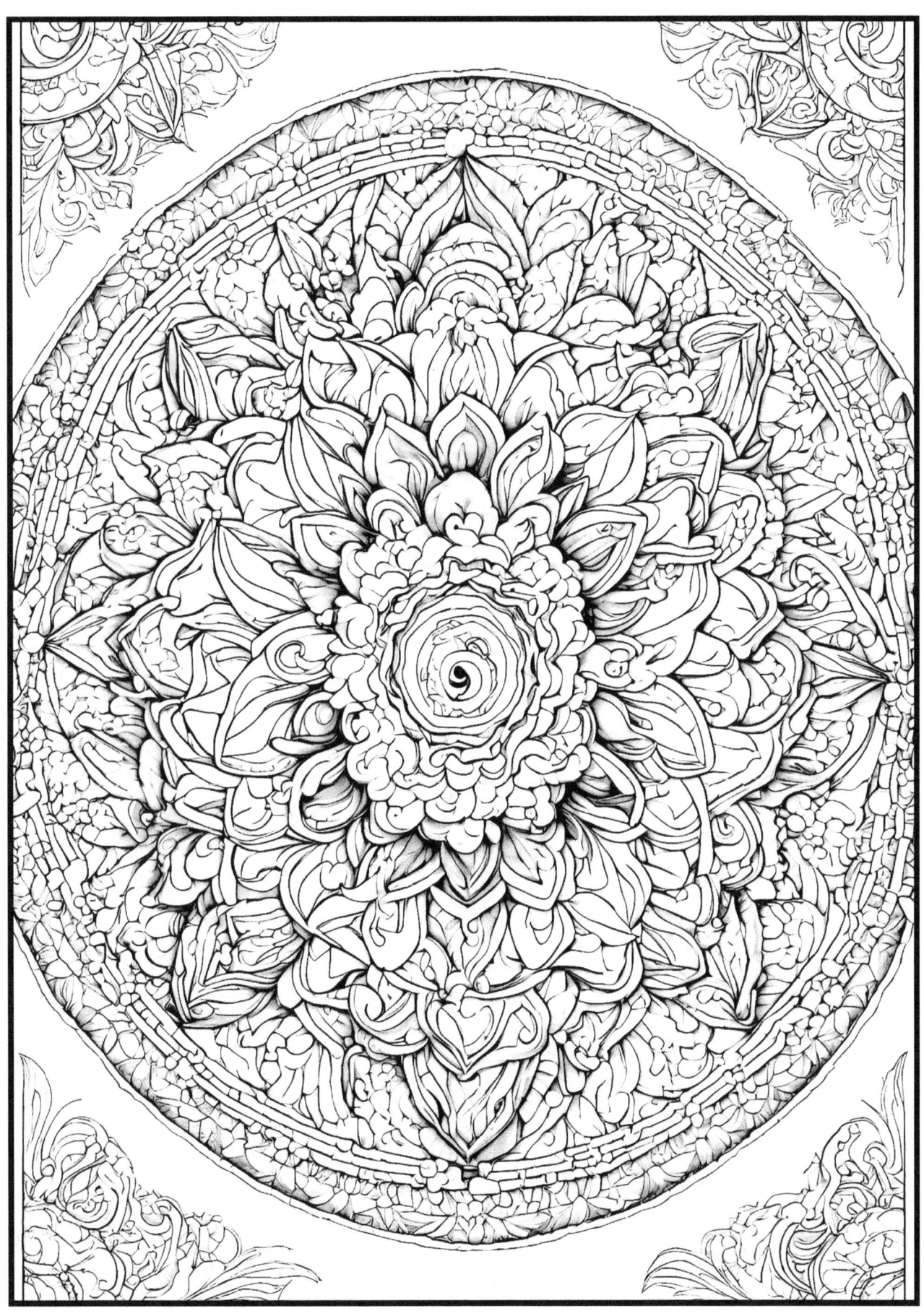

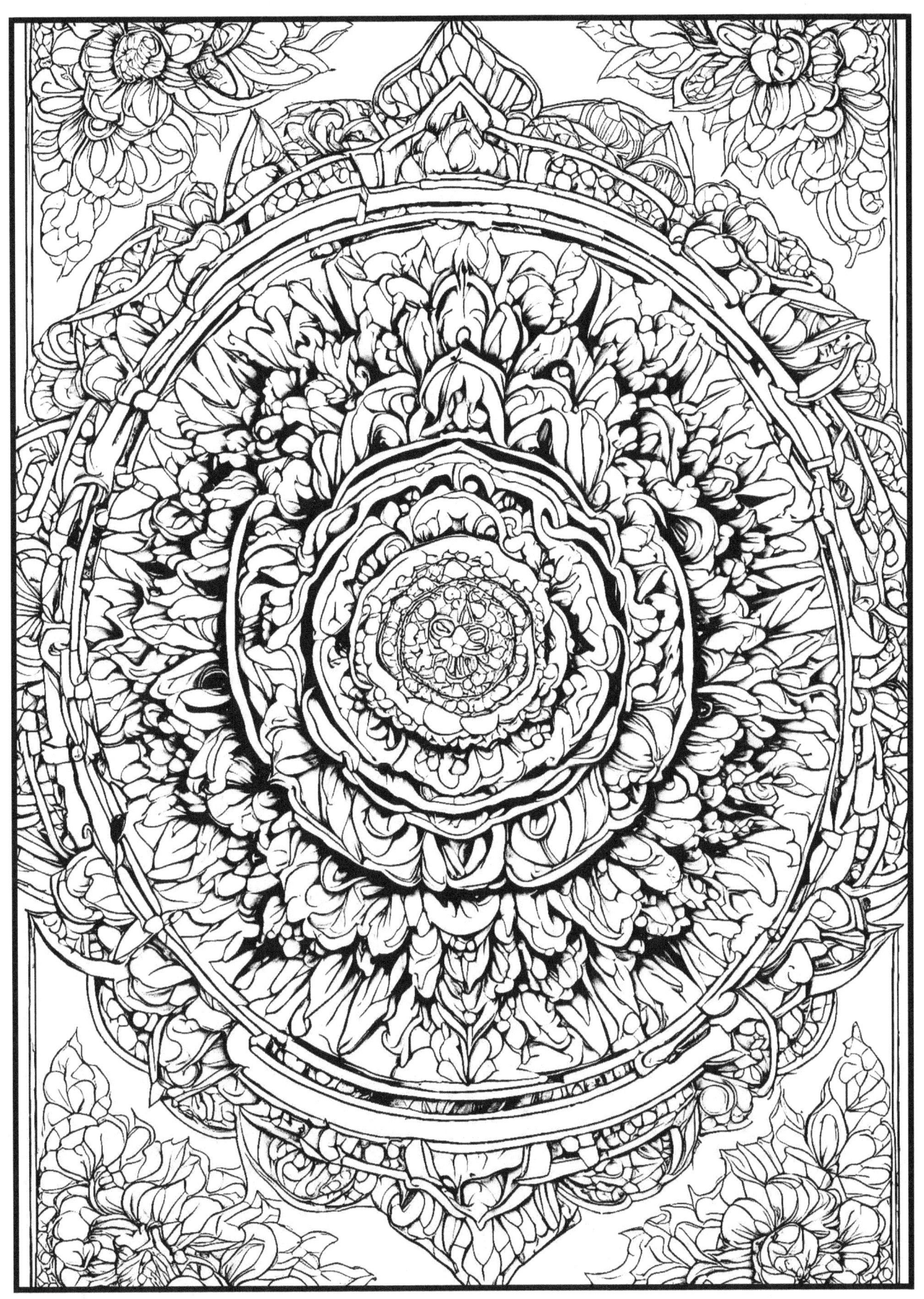

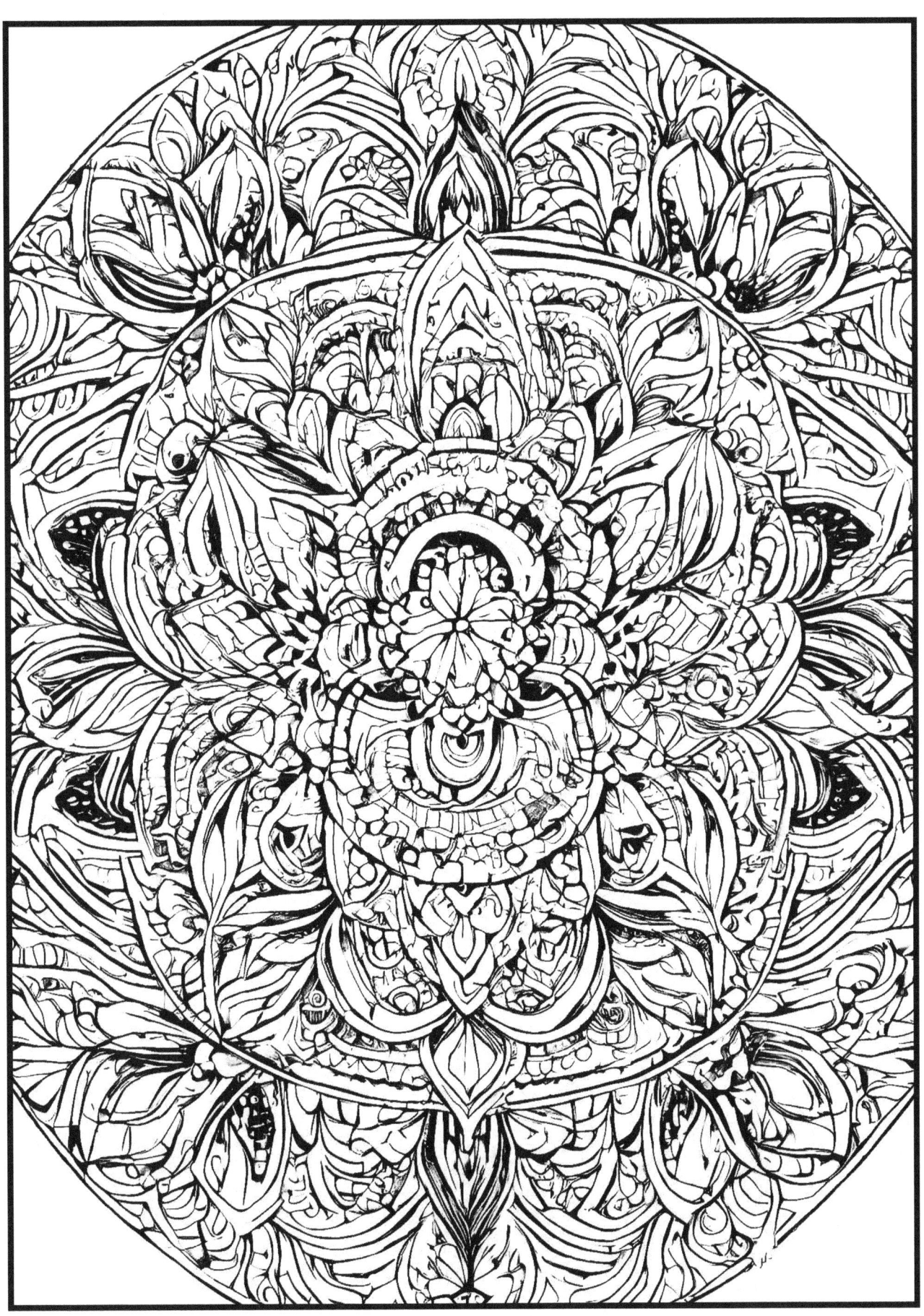

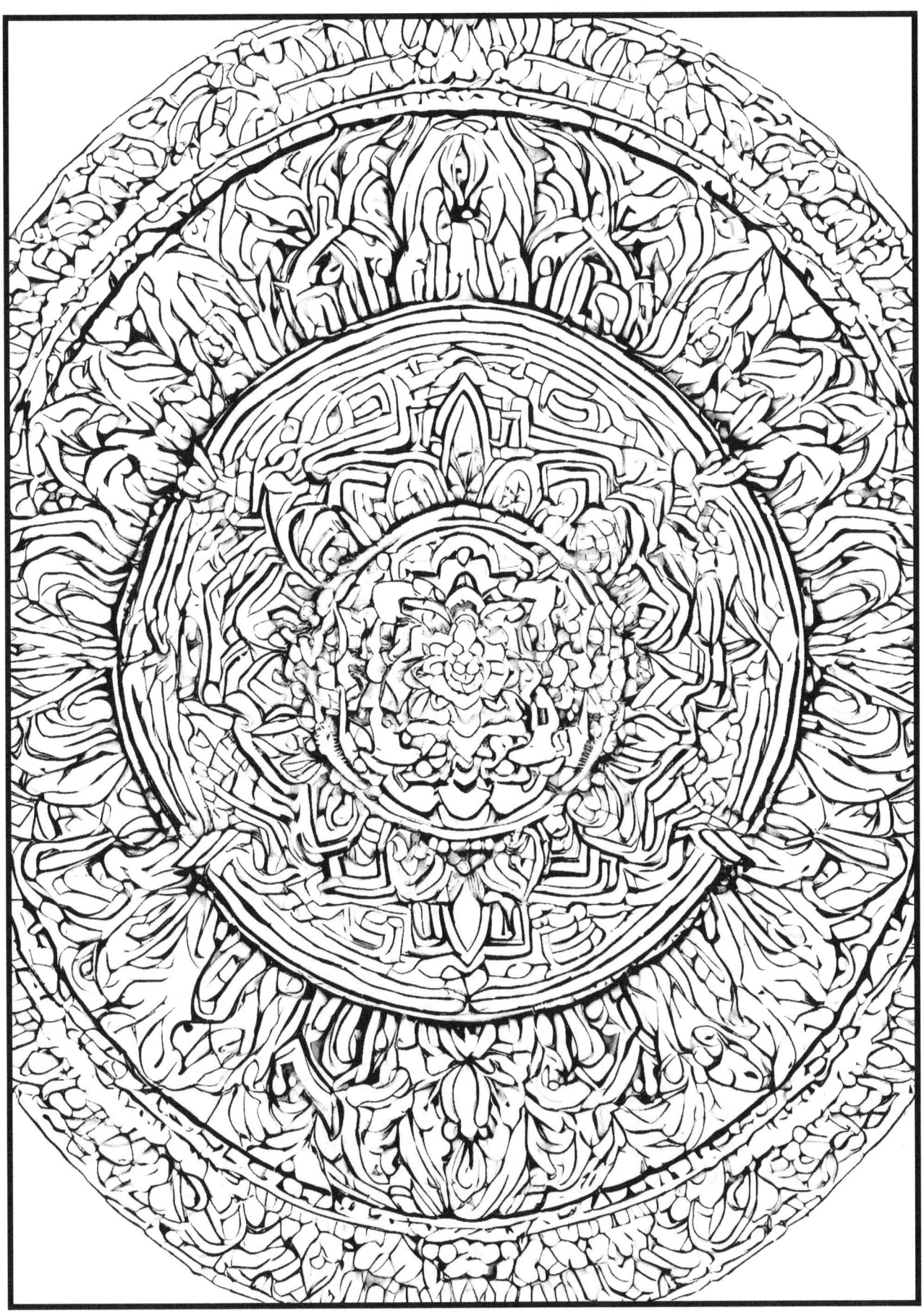

Dear Reader,

Thank you for choosing to read my book. Your support means the world to me. If you enjoyed this coloring book, would you mind leaving a review? Your feedback is invaluable to me as an author and helps others discover the book.

Warm regards,

Brooke E. Morgan